From Prophets and Lawgivers to 20th-Century America: How Came the Bible?

". . . they wrote it in Hebrew and Greek for one thing, and we read it in English. And, for another, its sixty-six books were not written all at once, to make up the Bible, but at intervals through fully a thousand years, and in places all the way from Babylon to Rome.

"How did these books come to find one another, and how did they come to possess the peculiar respect and authority so generally ascribed to them?"

— Edgar I. Goodspeed

The answers to the most fascinating mystery of all are here in this uncommon guide to the single common heritage of the Western World.

D1310716

How Came The Bible?

Edgar J. Goodspeed

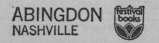
ABINGDON
NASHVILLE
festival books

HOW CAME THE BIBLE?

A FESTIVAL BOOK

Copyright 1940 by Edgar J. Goodspeed
Copyright © renewal 1968 by Foster B. Rhodes and
Stephen S. Goodspeed

Published by Pillar Books for Abingdon

Festival edition published April 1976

ISBN: 0-687-17524-0

Printed in the United States of America

TABLE OF CONTENTS

INTRODUCTION

An invitation from my old friend, Dr. Lucius H. Bugbee, to prepare a series of lessons on the formation, transmission and translation of the Bible resulted in a course of thirteen lessons under the title "The Growth of the Bible," to appear in the autumn issues of *The Adult Bible Class Monthly*, of this year. Doctor Bugbee and Doctor Langdale have now generously proposed that the lessons be gathered up in a volume, and I have been glad to act upon this suggestion.

These studies do not attempt to tell how the several books of the Bible came to be written; but only how, once written, they came to be gathered into the great religious libraries we know as the Old and New Testaments, and the Apocrypha, and how these have come down the centuries to our day. These are questions which rise in many thoughtful minds, and call for the best answers scholarship can find. The answers, so far as we can give them, form what seems to me a very interesting story.

EDGAR J. GOODSPEED.

Bel-Air, Los Angeles.

CHAPTER I
THE BOOKS OF THE BIBLE

THE English Bible is so omnipresent, on every pulpit and lectern, in every home, and even in almost every hotel room, that we are in some danger of taking it for granted, as one of the commonplaces of life. Yet as we grow older, it does sometimes occur to us to wonder how it came down to us; how it found its way, from the prophets and law-givers of Israel and the Christian apostles and evangelists, to us, in twentieth-century America.

For they wrote it in Hebrew and Greek for one thing, and we read it in English. And, for another, its sixty-six books were not written all at once, to make up the Bible, but at intervals through fully a thousand years, and in places all the way from Babylon to Rome. How did these books come to find one another and to be grouped together, and how did they come to possess the peculiar respect and authority so generally ascribed to them?

For, after all, as the thirty-nine books of the Old Testament were written one by one, they did not immediately rise into the dignity of Scripture. They found their way up to that level for the most part gradually, after a historical development in which they had proved their religious value. How and when did they begin to be so regarded, and what were the stages of the extraordinary development that gave the Old Testament, first to the Jewish people, and then to the Christian Church?

We must remember that an ancient book was in form a roll—as the Jews made them, scrolls of skin, finished smooth on one side to be written on. These might be of most inconvenient length; Jesus in the synagogue was handed "the roll of the prophet Isaiah," and he "found the place where it was written" —a difficult thing to do in the long series of columns of that book, which amounts in print to 125 large pages and must have made at least that many columns of Hebrew, with no chapter-numbers, capitals, or column numbers (there were no pages) to aid the reader in his search.

The Hebrew Bible—the Old Testament— as Jesus knew it, consisted of from twelve to twenty such scrolls of different sizes. They were never united into what we would call one "book" until the invention of printing made that possible, in the fifteenth century. Indeed, the sacred scriptures preserved in the arks of Jewish synagogues today are still scrolls, not leaf-books of the ordinary modern fashion.

So a "Bible" as we know it, even a Hebrew Bible, containing the Old Testament by itself, was unknown among the Jews of ancient times. The books that belonged to it were not physically united as they are with us; they existed in separate rolls or scrolls, one containing the Pentateuch, the first five books of the Old Testament; another, Isaiah (Luke 4. 17); another, the Minor Prophets (mentioned in Acts 7. 42); another, Ezekiel; another, the Psalms (referred to in Luke 20.42, and in Acts 1.20), and so on.

The Greeks made their rolls of papyrus, cutting the pith of that Egyptian water-plant into narrow strips and gluing these together into strips and these into sheets, which could then be glued together to make rolls of any length. But the Greeks had found that twenty-five to thirty feet was the length most convenient for ordinary use. Such a papyrus roll they called a *biblion*, from *biblos*, "papyrus." This is the word used of the Revelation, in Revelation 22. 18, 19, where it refers, of course, to the roll containing the Revelation alone. If it had referred to the whole New Testament (some books of which had not yet been written!) it would have been *plural*, biblia. Indeed, it was this plural which passed into Latin as a singular, *Biblia*, and came to mean the Bible. Etymologically, it means the papyrus rolls.

Can you recite the books of the Bible, in order?

Probably you can, with an effort, though you may get a little mixed on the Minor

Prophets and the minor Epistles. A clever woman recently offered to recite them for me at a dinner table. It is certainly a very useful piece of information to possess, especially when it comes to looking up references in Ecclesiastes or Habakkuk. But we must not jump to the conclusion that it is the only order in which the Bible has ever been arranged, as a missionary to Africa did in a recent letter to me. Still less that the books were written in this order, as some people hastily conclude.

The books of the Bible have appeared in a variety of orders, Hebrew, Greek, Latin, German, Swedish, Danish, English, and so on. And, of course, there is significance as well as convenience in all these orders.

In the Hebrew Bible the prophets, major and minor, follow Kings. After the last of them, Malachi, come what are sometimes called the poetical books, though the prophets were most of them poets too—Psalms, Proverbs, Job, the Song of Songs. Then come Ruth, Lamentations, Ecclesiastes, Esther and Daniel, and finally Ezra, Nehemiah, and Chronicles. This is a very significant order, for it reflects something of the growth of the Old Testament collection, which consisted first of Law, then of Law and Prophets, and then of Law, Prophets and Writings.

In the early Church, the Jewish scriptures were known, not in Hebrew, but in a Greek translation from it, called the Septuagint, from the seventy (*septuaginta*) elders credited by Jewish tradition with having made it. This Greek Old Testament has the thirty-nine books of the Hebrew Bible in another order, altogether different from the Hebrew one. The Jews arranged their biblical books in three groups—the Law, the Prophets and the Writings—and always kept them distinct. But in the Greek Bible these rigid boundaries were not maintained. The poetical books slipped in between the Former and the Latter Prophets; in fact, the third group, the Writings, disappeared altogether, its books being scattered through the other two groups.

Not only did the Greek Bible entirely upset the Hebrew order of the books; it actually added other books not found in the Hebrew at all, the so-called Apocrypha. These did not form a group by themselves, but were scattered through the Old Testament, Tobit and Judith (or Judith and Tobit) following Esther, and the Wisdom of Solomon and the Wisdom of Sirach following Job or the Song of Songs, and so forth. The oldest manuscripts of the Greek Bible, which come from the fourth and fifth centuries, do not agree in the order of the books, and put what we know as the Apocrypha in at various points.

The great Bible of the Middle Ages was the Vulgate, the Latin translation produced by Saint Jerome about the end of the fourth century, and based on the earlier Latin versions, which had sprung up anonymously in the second and third centuries, as Christianity began to reach Latin-speaking circles in the Roman Empire. The Latin manuscript copies have orders of their own which differ from the Greek and Hebrew orders and sometimes also from one another. Their usual order was at last fixed by the invention of printing, for the first large book printed was the 42-line Latin Bible, produced at Mainz about 1456.

But the Latin Bible had already been translated into German, in Bohemia, in the fourteenth century, and into English by Wyclif and his helpers in 1382 to 1388. Both these translations follow a Latin order, and have the Apocrypha scattered through the Old Testament. The later Catholic translation of the Old Testament made by Gregory Martin, in 1578 to 1582, and printed in 1610, was also made from the Latin translation—the Vulgate—and followed its order of books, with the Apocrypha distributed through the Old Testament.

Luther's new translation of the Bible into German, finished in 1534, was based on the Hebrew and Greek, and when he had finished the Greek New Testament (1522) and the Hebrew Old Testament, there still remained the books in the old Bibles that were in the

Latin Old Testament but not in the Hebrew. These Luther did last, as the Apocrypha, grouping them by themselves under that name, and putting them after the Old Testament. That Luther meant to do this must have become plain as the six parts of his Bible came out (1522-34), for Zwingli adopted the plan in his Swiss German Bible of 1530.

The first printed English Bible was that of Coverdale. It came out in 1535, a year after the appearance of Luther's Bible. Coverdale followed Luther in his rearrangement of the Old Testament, grouping the Apocryha together at the end of it. He also followed Luther in his bold rearrangement of the latter part of the New Testament. Luther valued biblical books in proportion as they "taught Christ." He felt that the Gospels did this best of all, but that there was least about Christ in Hebrews, James, Jude and the Revelation, and these he grouped together at the end of the New Testament, as least in religious value.

In this he was immediately followed by William Tyndale in his New Testament translation of 1525, the first to be printed in English. The Coverdale Bible of 1535 also followed Luther in this rearrangement of the latter part of the New Testament and it reappears in the John Rogers Bible of 1537.

But the Great Bible of 1539, the first Authorized English Bible, gave up this innovation of Luther's and adopted a more logical order, with Hebrews following the Letters of Paul, and James leading the list of the General Epistles. The Great Bible was also the first printed English Bible to put Jude last of the General Epistles, and was followed in this course by the Geneva Bible, the Bishops' Bible and the King James, as well as the Revised Versions, English and American.

A more startling variation in New Testament order was the putting of the Letters of Paul after the Gospels and before the Acts, in the great Sinaitic manuscript of the fourth century, found by Tischendorf in a convent on Mount Sinai in 1859 and now in the British Museum. This manuscript contains the oldest complete Greek New Testament we possess, and reminds us of the fact that readers of the New Testament in the second and third centuries did not have it in a single volume but in four or five leaf-books, or if they used it in roll-form, probably in as many as eight rolls or scrolls. There might well be some variety of opinion as to the order in which these various smaller collections of books were to be arranged when put together.

The older Greek manuscripts, for example,

put the General Epistles James, Peter, John, and Jude, after the Acts, but English New Testaments and Bibles from Tyndale down almost without exception put them, or at least five of them, after the Letters of Paul.

There was even uncertainty or a least variety in the order of the Gospels. The famous Codex of Beza, so called because it once belonged to that great French Reformer, has them in the order Matthew—John—Luke—Mark. This manuscript was written in the sixth century. The fifth-century manuscript of the Gospels bought in Egypt by Mr. Freer, of Detroit, in 1906, and now in the Smithsonian Institution in Washington, has the Gospels in the same order, Matthew—John—Luke—Mark. Other orders of the Gospels appear in some manuscripts, though the familiar order is pretty certainly the original one.

So the ancient and modern Bibles reveal a good deal of variety in the order of the sixty-six books that compose it—neglecting for the present the books of the Apocrypha, which formed part of the Old Testament regularly from the first century to the seventeenth, and usually until the beginning of the nineteenth. But these variations mostly had to do with minor books. The broad lines of the arrangement were tolerably fixed. The Old Testament began with the great historical series, from Genesis to Second Kings—from creation to B. C. 561; and the New, with the four Gospels and the Acts, followed by the Epistles, Pauline and general, and closing usually with the Revelation.

This variation is of most significance to us as reminding us that until modern times the Bible was not usually one book, but a whole shelf of books, which might be arranged in various ways. They were written in the course of a thousand years, by some forty writers, scattered over two thousand miles of distance, all the way from Babylon to Rome. And once written, how did they find one another, and come to form our Bible? This is the question that sometimes comes to our minds as we explore this vast and varied religious literature we call The Bible.

QUESTIONS

1. What was the form of the Bible in Jesus' day? ~~scroll~~ roll or scrolls 12 – 20 scrolls

2. What was the origin of the name "Bible"? Bible

3. What were the main groups of books in the Hebrew Bible? Prophets, major + minor,

- 4. In what form did the early Christians use it? form

5. What additions were made to it? Putting pages together

6. What change did Luther make in the old Testament order? He grouped by name after the O.T.

7. What effect did this have on the English Bible? it caused a more logical order: greater arrangements

8. On what principle is the first half of our Old Testament arranged? *historical series* (Page 19)

9. Has there been any variation in the order of New Testament books? *yes ; Page 18*

Biblion

Kings, malachi, Psalms, Proverbs, Job Song of Solmo- Ruth, Lamentation, Ecclesiastes, Esther, Daniel, Ezra, nehemiah & chronicles : Law, Prophets + writings

CHAPTER II

THE BEGINNING OF THE OLD
TESTAMENT

PROBABLY the oldest piece of literature in the Old Testament is the war song in the fifth chapter of Judges, known as the Song of Deborah. It belongs to the twelfth century before Christ. The narratives of the prophetic historians of the Northern and the Southern kingdoms, of Israel and Judah, arose in the ninth and eighth centuries before Christ. In the eighth century the literary prophets began to appear, Amos and Hosea, Micah and Isaiah, that great quartette, who wrote their brilliant prophetic poetry between 765 and 701 B. C.

Prized and valued as their writings were, there is nothing to suggest that they were thought of as sacred, or scripture, and after the death of Isaiah, who probably suffered martyrdom when the half-heathen king Manasseh came to the throne, there was no prophecy in Judah. The prophets were silenced or killed. The worship of Jehovah was neglected, and religion sank to a low ebb.

The accession of Josiah and his eagerness to restore the worship of Jehovah led to the renovation of the Temple, and in the course of this, in B. C. 621, the book of Deuteronomy was discovered. The priest took it to the king, who joyfully welcomed it and set about putting its program of religious reformation into effect. The dramatic story is told in 2 Kings 22 and 23. Josiah put a stop to the idolatrous practices of the people, ordered the offering of sacrifice to be confined to the city of Jerusalem, and required the Passover celebration to be held there. These are all definitely prescribed in Deuteronomy.

So Deuteronomy became the law of the land. It had been written in the dark, idolatrous days of Manasseh, by some prophet in hiding from the king and his officers, who, since he could not preach, wrote his message, in the hope that a time would come when it might be found and heeded. And this unknown prophet came to exercise a great influence on Jewish religion and Jewish literature.

Deuteronomy is the fusion of the two great forces in Jewish religious life, the priestly and the prophetic. The priests cared for sacrifice, ritual and ceremonial; the prophets were concerned with moral uprightness and the inner life. In Deuteronomy these two interests were nobly combined, and the priestly ritual was made the symbol and vehicle of the spiritual religion. It is true, worship became less personal and individual, and more national; the little private local sacrifices and worships had to be given up. The reason for this was that it was in them that old idolatrous practices often continued, or new idolatries crept in. The writer of Deuteronomy felt that if sacrifice and worship were confined to Jerusalem, they could be controlled and protected from adulteration.

So Deuteronomy represents the triumph of the prophets over the old idolatry and the foreign worships that occasionally crept in. It grew out of still older Hebrew codes of law— the Book of the Covenant, still preserved in Exodus 20. 22 to 23. 33, which probably reflects the reform of Asa, king of Judah, about B. C. 900. And this in turn grew out of a still more primitive set of laws, the Little Book of the Covenant, Exodus 34, which seems to have been the germ of the Hebrew legislation.

But Deuteronomy was the first presentation of the Hebrew law in anything resembling a book, and this book became the kernel of the Old Testament. Those were the days of a new group of literary prophets, Zephaniah, Nahum, Jeremiah, and Habakkuk, who wrote their prophecies between the Scythian invasion of 627 and the destruction of Jerusalem by the Babylonians in 586.

The overthrow of Judah and the destruction of the Temple were followed by long years of exile, which were most depressing nationally but very fruitful from a religious point of view. Following the lines marked out by Jeremiah, Ezekiel declared that religion was personal instead of national, and pointed out the religious responsibility of the individual. Exiled Jews turned to their law as a subject for study and enrichment, and the histories that had been written in the ninth and eighth centuries in Judah and Israel were now united with Deuteronomy to form a greater law. For the study and preservation of this the synagogue arose, and Judaism was enabled to survive the destruction of its Temple and the interruption of its national worship. For the Jews, deprived of their capital and Temple, now rallied around their law.

The Law reached its full stature soon after B. C. 400, when it was again enlarged, by combining with it a priestly history and legislation that had grown up in the preceding century. Leviticus, the book of the priestly law, was the principal addition it made to the Law, but every part of the old collection was also enriched. The result was a work of magnificent scope and of epic quality. It was an outline of history, an account of the beginnings of human institutions and nations, a system of worship and a manual of religion and morals—all in one. This was the Pentateuch.

The reverence that had attached to Deuteronomy from its discovery in B. C. 621 extended to the whole huge book, which was almost as long as the New Testament. Wherever the Jews wandered, they organized synagogues and read and studied the Law. It became their supreme treasure. When the Samaritans formed their branch of Judaism, around B. C. 400, they took with them the Law, and ancient copies of it, written in Samaritan characters, are still treasured in their community in Nablus—the "Samaritan Pentateuch." The fact that the Samaritans never accepted any other books of Jewish scripture shows that, when they broke off from Judaism, that was all the scripture there was. It reflects the stage of development the Jewish scriptures had reached at the time of that event.

The Samaritan group owed its origin to a romantic incident in the family of the Jewish high priest. One of his sons had married a foreign wife, the daughter of Sanballat the Horonite (Nehemiah 13. 28). Nehemiah and Ezra gave orders that all such marriages be annulled, and such foreign wives and their children be driven out. But this young priest refused to disown his wife, and so he was expelled from the Jewish community. But his father-in-law, Sanballat, built him a temple on Mount Gerizim, near Shechem, the modern Nablus, and the Samaritan sect was the result.

The Law was the first part of the Jewish scriptures to be translated into Greek, when

the Septuagint version was begun in Egypt
about the middle of the third century before
Christ. The whole Law would make a roll too
bulky and clumsy to suit Greek book-habits,
and so they divided the Law into five rolls, 88
and gave them the names we know them by—
Genesis, Exodus, Leviticus, Numbers, Deuteronomy. Fragments of a Greek papyrus
roll of Deuteronomy, written about the middle of the second century before Christ, were
discovered and published by the Rylands
Library of Manchester, England, four years
ago. This is probably the oldest piece of Biblical text now known.

The Sadducees, so well known to us from
the part they play in the Gospels, also accepted only the Law as scripture. The Phar- 89
isees did not stop there, but in their attach-
ment to the Law they were devout to the
verge of fanaticism. Before and after touch-
ing a copy of it one must wash his hands;
as they picturesquely put it, the Law defiled
the hands. This quaint tribute they afterward
paid to all their scriptures.

The persecutions directed by Antiochus
Epiphanes against the Jews in the Maccabean times included the copies of the Law,
which the Jews were ordered to surrender, so
that they could be destroyed. "Wherever they
found the Book of the Law, they tore them up
and burned them." Anyone who possessed
a copy was condemned to death (1 Maccabees

1. 56, 57). The Law had become the symbol of the Jewish religion.

As Hebrew was gradually displaced by Aramaic as the language of everyday life, when the Law was read in the synagogue it had to be translated into Aramaic, to be understood. This was done verse by verse. In the first century after Christ an Aramaic translation or Targum of the Law was produced, but it was not committed to writing; it was preserved orally, being memorized by one generation of scribes after another. The scribes had first arisen as the copyists of the Law, as their name indicates. But they became its custodians and interpreters. In the first century they also produced a Hebrew commentary on the Law, but it too could not be written; it must be memorized, for to write it would seem to put it on a level with "what was written"—the Law itself. These strange proceedings, as we consider them, show the extreme reverence with which the Jews of the Pharisaic type had come to regard the Law.

In ancient Jewish synagogues there was an "ark" or cupboard for the accommodation of the scroll of the Law, just as there is today. In fact, it is not too much to say that the Law almost occupied the place and was shown the reverence an idol would have had in a pagan temple. The primary function of the synagogue was instruction in the Law.

The Law is much talked of in the Gospels (Matthew, Luke, John) and in the letters of Paul. Jesus created a great sensation when, in his words about clean and unclean food, he swept the whole Levitical legislation away— the characteristic priestly contribution to the Law (Mark 7. 19). On the other hand, Jesus saw enduring values in the Law, and asserted them in no uncertain terms:

"I tell you, as long as heaven and earth endure, not one dotting of an *i* or crossing of a *t* will be dropped from the Law until it is all observed" (Matthew 5. 18).

QUESTIONS

1. What was the origin of Deuteronomy?
2. What were its chief features?
3. What was the effect of the Exile upon the development of the Jewish Law?
4. What additions did Deuteronomy receive?
5. When did the Law reach its final form?
6. Why have the Samaritans only the Law?
7. What was the origin of their branch of Judaism?
8. What happened to the Law when it was put into Greek?
9. How did the Pharisees show their extreme respect for the Law?
10. What part does the Law play in the New Testament?
11. What is your favorite passage in the Law?

CHAPTER III
THE LAW AND THE PROPHETS

When the Jews settled upon the Law as the guide of their social and religious lives, they already had a wealth of other religious writings of the finest kind. The great literary prophets had all spoken and written—Amos, Hosea, Micah, and Isaiah in the eighth century; Zephaniah, Nahum, Habakkuk, and Jeremiah in the seventh; Ezekiel, Haggai, and Zechariah in the sixth; Malachi, Obadiah and Joel in the fifth. The history of the Kingdom, which we know as the four books of Samuel and Kings, was finally completed in the sixth century, and the book of Judges was finished in the fifth.

To the modern reader, the religious value of this literature, especially of the prophets, seems greater than that of the books of the Jewish Law, and the Jews themselves were not long in coming to a recognition of their religious usefulness.

The historical books they recognized as religious and therefore prophetic in purpose, and these they grouped with the book of Joshua into what they called the Former Prophets—Joshua, Judges, Samuel, and Kings. The second part of the prophetic collection was the Latter Prophets, and contained Isaiah, Jeremiah, Ezekiel, and the

"Book of the Twelve," or as we call them the Minor Prophets—Hosea to Malachi. But, as the Jews reckoned, the Latter Prophets were four in number, like the Former Prophets. The twelve Minor Prophets together would not fill a scroll as long as that containing Isaiah, and that is why they were grouped in this way and counted as one. Four scrolls would hold the Former Prophets and four the Latter.

Of course the books they described as the Former Prophets were really written later than some of the Latter Prophets, but they named them as they did in view of the times they dealt with. Who wrote the Former Prophets they did not pretend to know, nor do we. Judges, Samuel, and Kings were all strongly influenced by Deuteronomy, but their authors are forgotten. The literature of Western Asia was mostly anonymous, in Israel as in Babylonia and Assyria. The remarkable thing is that, in the case of the literary prophets, so many writers' names were recorded and preserved.

Sometimes between B. C. 250 and 175 this collection of the prophets was formed and came to be recognized as authoritative, side by side with the Law. In four hundred or four hundred and fifty years the Bible of Judaism had grown from the book of Deuteronomy to the Law and the Prophets. By the time of Jesus lessons from both the Law

and the Prophets were read every Sabbath
in the synagogue, and were translated into
Aramaic for those for whom Hebrew had
become a dead language. But the Prophets
were never recognized as quite equal to the
Law, for the Law was translated verse by
verse, but the Prophets three verses at a
time.

We have seen that in Deuteronomy the prophetic and priestly ideals of religion were
blended and harmonized. When the Law was
expanded to the great work we know as
the Pentateuch—Genesis to Deuteronomy—
the priestly element came to predominate;
Leviticus was very priestly in color. But the
balance between the priestly and the prophetic was now restored, with the acceptance of
the eight books of the prophets.

We are familiar with the idea that it was
the prophets that prepared the way for Jesus,
and to the Christian mind, the work of the
prophets appeals as much more deeply religious than that of the priests. It was, in fact,
the distinctive thing about the Jewish religion. The prophets are still influencing the
world, and will, we hope, do so increasingly
as the years go by. For they struck down to
the great realities of spiritual religion which
do not grow old.

Amos and Micah, in the eighth century,
denounced social and economic injustice, and
proclaimed the justice of God. With these

prophets we are introduced to what has been called the ethical monotheism of the prophets —their great religious discovery that God was the God of all nations, and that he was impartially just. The same justice, they declared, must prevail among men, or the wrath of God would be poured out upon them, whether they were Jews or pagans.

To their times belongs Hosea, the great prophet of the indefatigable, unfailing love of God. This great religious idea which was to reach its fulness in Christianity, is the necessary supplement of the idea of the divine justice. It makes room for God's mercy and forgiveness.

Amos and Micah were peasants, but Isaiah was a man of position and influence in Jerusalem. He knew the king, and did not hesitate to warn and advise him. This brings us to one of the leading traits of the prophets; they were fearless critics of the society they lived in. Their value to it lay in the fact that they could see its faults, and correct them.

To the great ideas of the justice and the love of God, Isaiah added the thought of the divine holiness, which carried with it the demand for holiness on the part of his people.

Two or three generations later, in 627, the young prophet Zephaniah saw in the approach of the Scythian hordes, who were coming down from the north, the prelude to the awful Day of the Lord, the day of judgment for Philistia, Egypt, Assyria—and Judah too. The history of their times is clearly reflected in the poems of these brilliant prophets. Zephaniah's contemporary Nahum, in particular, described the fall of Nineveh with a dramatic detail that brings the scene vividly before the modern reader.

But the fall of Nineveh and the end of the Assyrian Empire, which had threatened Judah so long, simply made room for a new tyrant, Babylonia, and Habakkuk gloomily wondered if this series of cruel oppressors was to go on forever. Jeremiah witnessed the capture and destruction of Jerusalem, but it led him to perceive that religion is not just a national, but a personal matter, and he and Ezekiel worked out the idea that religion and moral responsibility are individual concerns.

It was this great perception that enabled Judaism to survive the downfall of the Jewish nation and the Temple worship, which would have put an end to any merely national religion. Even the deportation of the Jews to Babylonia and their stay there for sixty years and more did not extinguish their religion. And when at last Babylon fell and Cyrus, the Persian king, allowed them to return, prophets like Haggai and Zechariah encouraged them to rebuild the Temple and resume their worship.

In the discouraging years that followed,

the prophets again and again reanimated the people, Malachi stirring them to greater devotion, Obadiah pointing out God's judgment upon the Edomites for their treatment of their Jewish brethren, and Joel reviving the people's hopes in the midst of drought and famine.

Hardly less useful to Jewish spiritual life were the books of Samuel and Kings, with their record of the religious experience of the nation and its leaders—kings like David, Hezekiah, and Josiah, and prophets like Samuel, Elijah, and Elisha. These books, with Joshua and Judges, they called the Former Prophets.

The reverence with which these historical books now came to be treated also illustrates the pious satisfaction with which the Jews, in their present reduced political and economic position, looked back upon the great days of their nation's history, its heroic period, when it had a place among the nations of the earth, and had such kings as David and Solomon.

So both patriotic and religious purposes were served when to the account in the Law, of human history from the creation to the finding of the Promised Land, was now added the continuation of the history through the days of the Conquest (Joshua), the Judges, and the Kings.

The Jewish Bible was also greatly enriched

in a literary way, for most of the literary prophets were poets, and the Latter Prophets formed a collection of Hebrew poetry of extraordinary brilliance and variety.

The Jewish Bible took on greatly increased religious depth and power when the books of the prophets were added to the Law. Its new name, the Law and the Prophets, meets us again and again in the New Testament— Paul, Matthew, Luke, John. See Matthew 7. 12—"For this is the law and the prophets." Luke mentions the reading of the Law and the Prophets as a regular part of the service in the Jewish synagogue in Pisidian Antioch. It preceded the sermon or appeal, which Paul was invited to give there (Acts 13. 15). Until John came, Jesus told the Pharisees, it was the Law and the Prophets, but now the kingdom of God was being proclaimed (Luke 16. 16). Paul wrote to the Romans that the Christian way of salvation had witness borne to it by the Law and the Prophets (Romans 3. 21). The prophets had promised it (Romans 1. 2).

While both Law and Prophets are often quoted in the New Testament, it was the prophetic strain in Jewish religion that revived and expanded in Christianity. The message of Jesus had in it much more of the prophet than of the priest. People saw in him a new prophet. "A great prophet has appeared among us," said the people of Nain (Luke 7.

16). When Jesus entered Jerusalem, the people cried, "It is Jesus, the prophet of Nazareth, in Galilee!" (Matthew 21. 11.) And Jesus accepted the rôle of prophet when he declared that he must go on to Jerusalem, "For it is not right for a prophet to die outside Jerusalem!" (Luke 13. 33.) Jesus found the keynote and the program for his work in the words of Isaiah, beginning (Luke 4. 18) :

"The spirit of the Lord is upon me,
For he has consecrated me to preach the
good news to the poor!"

He gathered a close circle of disciples about him, as Isaiah had done (Isaiah 8. 16), and he applied to the Jewish people the words of discouragement and rebuke that Isaiah had used,

"This nation's mind has grown dull,
And they hear faintly with their ears,
And they have shut their eyes,
So as never to see with their eyes,
And hear with their ears,
And understand with their minds, and turn
back,
And let me cure them!" (Matthew 13. 15.)

While the Jews counted the Latter Prophets as four books, we count them as fifteen, for their Book of the Twelve Prophets we count as twelve. Joshua, Judges, Samuel, and Kings form six books as we know them, so that the Former and Latter Prophets added no less than twenty-one books to the Jewish Scriptures, as we count them. And this great numerical increase in Jewish sacred books is only a symbol of the great spiritual re-enforcement the Books of the Prophets brought to the Jewish, and later to the Christian, religion.

QUESTIONS

1. In what four centuries did the work of the prophets fall? *P 8034*
2. What did the Jews include under "the Former Prophets"? *P 30*
3. Why did they class these books as prophets?
4. What books made up "the Latter Prophets"? *P 30*
5. Why were they called "Latter"? *P 31*
6. What prophetic writers were included in the Latter Prophets? *P 36*
7. What great religious ideas were embodied in these books? *P 32*
8. What use was made of the prophets in the synagogue service?
9. How does the New Testament link up with the prophets? *P 36*
10. Were the Jewish prophets mostly prose writers, or mostly poets? *P 36*
11. What is your favorite passage in the Prophets?

Matt 7:12
21:11

CHAPTER IV

THE COMPLETION OF THE OLD TESTAMENT

THE expansion of the Jewish Scriptures, as the Pharisees viewed them, did not stop with the addition of the Prophets to the Law. The Jews had long been developing a rich practical and devotional literature of hymns and precepts, sermons and short stories. Among the stories, Ruth, Esther and Jonah are pre-eminent; Jonah had already found a place in the Book of the Twelve Prophets. Philosophical discussions of religion, like Job and Ecclesiastes, dirges like Lamentations, love poetry like the Song of Songs, show the variety of this later literature. There was also the priestly rewriting of the nation's history, that we know as the books of Chronicles, an ecclesiastical chronicle of Jerusalem, as it has been called, based upon the earlier histories, in the Former Prophets, but omitting the accounts of the monarchs of Israel, the Northern kingdom.

The great central unit in this secondary religious literature however was the book of Psalms. It was both the hymnbook and the prayerbook of the Second Temple, the Temple after the Exile. As we have it, it is a collection of collections, for four hymns are repeated in it; 14 is the same as 53; 40. 13-17 is the same as 70; 57. 7-11 and 60. 5-12 are the same as 108. These hymns were evidently in more than one of the collections or minor hymnbooks that were put together to make our Psalter.

The prominence, even dominance, of the Psalms in this third part of the Old Testament shows us why the full Jewish scripture is sometimes spoken of, as in Luke 24. 44, as the Law, the Prophets, and the Psalms.

The Psalms have a great deal to tell us about the situations and periods in which they arose, but our chief interest in them is as expressions of personal religious life— remorse, repentance, aspiration, communion, hope, faith, confidence. No book in the Bible is so dear to modern devotion as the Psalms. What book in the whole Old Testament means so much to your own religion as it does?

The earliest reference to this enlargement of the Jewish Scripture by the addition of a third body of books is in the preface to the Wisdom of Sirach. Jeshua, or Jesus, son of Sirach, was a Jewish sage who composed his Wisdom toward the end of the third century before Christ, or early in the second. He wrote in Hebrew, but fifty years later his grandson down in Egypt translated his book into Greek, prefixing to it a few lines of explanation. In this preface he speaks of the Law, the Prophecies and the rest of the books, as already translated into Greek, and as illustrating the difficulty of translating Hebrew into that language.

So the third part of the Old Testament was already taking shape and being added to the Law and the Prophets in the second century before Christ; in fact, it was already being translated into Greek, for the use of Jews in Egypt who knew Greek better than Hebrew, and also for missionary purposes.

This third section of Jewish scripture was not finally fixed and settled, however, until about the close of the first century after Christ, when in the Jewish Synod of Jamnia, about A. D. 90, what few uncertainties there were about it were officially settled.

The Psalms were quoted in 1 Maccabees, 7. 17, a work written early in the last century before Christ. Job and Proverbs were associated with them. To these were added what were called the Five Rolls—the Song of Songs, Ruth, Lamentations, Ecclesiastes and Esther, which are read one on each of the five Jewish festivals: the Song of Songs at the Passover, Ruth at Pentecost (the Harvest festival), Lamentations on the anniversary of the destruction of Jerusalem, Ecclesiastes at Tabernacles (the Camping-out festival), and Esther at Purim, the origin of which it seeks to explain.

The final group in this third division of the Jewish Bible consisted of Daniel, Ezra-Nehe-

miah, and Chronicles, making a total of
twenty-four books, as the Jews counted them,
a figure which corresponded to the number
of letters in the Hebrew alphabet, which can
be counted as twenty-two or twenty-four.
This probably suggested to the Jewish mind
an impression of fixity and completeness.
There was no room for any additions, and
so the scripture collection might be considered
safe from alteration.

They arrived at this total however in various ways, which seem strange to us. Sometimes they counted Ruth as part of Judges,
Nehemiah as part of Ezra, and Lamentations
as part of Jeremiah. Samuel, Kings, and
Chronicles, of course, were one book each.
The twelve Minor Prophets formed one book
or roll, as we have seen, and this made a total
of twenty-two books. Or they sometimes
counted the Song of Songs, Ruth, Lamentations, Ecclesiastes, and Esther as one book
(for they could all be gotten into a single
scroll), and still reached the same total,
which seems to have been an important point.

By the time Josephus wrote his two books
Against Apion, late in the first century after
Christ, this was the state of the Jewish development of scripture. Josephus recognized
five books of Moses, that is, the Law; thirteen
books by the prophets, while "the remaining
four books contain hymns to God and precepts
for the conduct of human life" (1. 8). By

this last he probably means Psalms, Job, Proverbs, and Ecclesiastes.

Almost every writer in the New Testament shows the use of the Psalms. Some of them drew heavily upon them. Jesus himself quoted from them again and again: Matthew 7. 23; 22. 44; 23. 39. Once at least he quoted them as scripture—"David under the Spirit's influence . . . says" (Matthew 22. 43). The hymn that Jesus and his disciples sang after the Last Supper was the Hallel, Psalms 113 to 118, part of which was sung early in the Passover supper, and part at the end.

Some of the latest products of Jewish religious experience were included in this part of the Jewish Bible. Ecclesiastes was written in the first half of the second century before Christ, the period that witnessed the completion of the Psalter, as we have it. Daniel sprang out of the persecution of the Jews by the king of Syria, to whom they were then subject, which resulted in the Maccabean uprising and triumph, around B. C. 165. It is repeatedly quoted in Matthew 24, and evidently as scripture: "When you see the dreadful desecration, of which the prophet Daniel spoke, set up in the Holy Place" (24. 15). No less than sixty-six reflections of the language of Daniel have been counted in the book of Revelation, on which its influence was very great.

This third part of the Jewish Bible made

room for the work of the more philosophical or humanistic type of Jewish thinkers, the wise men, or sages. As Moses was the model of the prophets, and David of the psalmists, Solomon was the ideal of the sages. Their goal was Wisdom, which they regarded as the highest good. Proverbs, Ecclesiastes, and the book of Job represented their work, in the Hebrew Bible. Like the prophets, the sages were poets, and sometimes poets of tremendous power, like the author of Job, whose richness of vocabulary and splendor of imagination have seldom been equaled in any literature.

But dearer to the modern religious heart are the hymns of the spirit, the devotional poetry of the Psalms. They still form our Classics of Devotion—the First, the Nineteenth, the Twenty-third, the Ninetieth, and many more. The Song of Songs represents poetry of a very different kind, the love songs of courtship and marriage, such as might be heard at Oriental weddings, like that described in 1 Maccabees 9. 35-42, or in Matthew, chapter 25. Ezra-Nehemiah brought Jewish history down from the end of the Exile to the reforms of Nehemiah and of Ezra, who began their work in Judea in B. C. 444 and 397, respectively.

In old English Bibles we often find the hymnbook bound up with the Bible, and something like this occurred when the Jews added their hymnbook to their scriptures, And how greatly it enriched those scriptures! The Psalms were the work of many hands and hearts, scattered over centuries of the most varied personal and national experience. It is the variety as well as the sincerity of these expressions that makes the Psalms such an inexhaustible mine of religious wealth. No one experiences all it has to give, but it has something for everyone. The inmost experiences, whether of despair or of aspiration, the great note of trust, the experience of worship—these and a score of other religious expressions are here in their highest form. One psalmist exults in his book of religion (119) another finds delight in the processionals and liturgies of the Temple. No book in the Bible speaks more widely and directly to our modern spiritual life, than this old Hebrew prayerbook and hymnbook, which gathers up the prayer and praise of so many worshiping hearts and makes us share in their practice of the presence of God. For of all the books of the Old Testament, religion becomes most personal in the Psalms.

So this last addition to the Hebrew Scriptures of Palestine covered Jewish philosophy, wisdom, ethics, devotion, liturgy, history, and love poetry. And in it we are introduced to the last phase of historical Judaism—the rise of the scribes, for the last historical figure it presents is Ezra the Scribe, reading the Law to the congregation (Nehemiah 8. 13, 18). With Ezra, the Jews liked to believe, the formation of their Scripture reached its end. We shall meet this idea again as we pursue the further growth of Jewish scripture outside of Palestine.

The Hebrew Bible then contained first the Law, in five books; the Former and the Latter Prophets, in four books each; and the Writings—Psalms, Job, Proverbs; the Five Rolls, comprising the Song of Songs, Ruth, Lamentations, Ecclesiastes, and Esther; and finally, Daniel, Ezra-Nehemiah and Chronicles. The doubts that remained about the Song of Songs and still more about Ecclesiastes vanished by the end of the first century after Christ.

QUESTIONS

1. What short stories now found a place in the Hebrew Bible?
2. How did the books of Chronicles differ from the narratives of Samuel and Kings?
3. What was the origin of the book of Psalms?
4. What is its modern religious value?
5. When did this enlargement of the Jewish scripture take place?
6. What is our first intimation of it?
7. When was it completed?
8. What did it include?

9. What new literary and religious elements did it bring into the Hebrew Bible?

10. Which of these books are reflected in the New Testament?

11. What book of the Old Testament makes the greatest contribution to personal religion?

12. What were the contents of the Jewish scriptures, as the Jews grouped them?

13. What is your favorite among the "Writings"?

CHAPTER V
THE APOCRYPHA

WHEN the Jews of Palestine limited the contents of their scripture to the books we know as the Old Testament, the Greek-speaking Jewish who lived in Egypt did not stop there. There had grown up among them a considerable group of other historical and religious writings, partly by translation of new works of Hebrew literature, partly by the enlargement of Old Testament books, like Esther and Daniel, in the course of translating them into Greek, and partly by original composition in Greek. These books became associated in Egypt with the translated Old Testament books, and so formed part of the Greek Old Testament, the so-called Septuagint version. And when this became the Bible of the early Church, these books went with it.

So the Apocrypha, as we call them, appear scattered through the Greek Bible of the early Church, and then through the Latin Bible, before and after Jerome's work of revising it. They passed naturally, as we have seen, into the early German translation of the Latin Bible, made in Bohemia in the fourteenth century, and also into the English translation made by Wyclif and his helpers, in 1382-88.

But Luther translated the Greek New

Testament and the Hebrew Old Testament;
and when he had finished these, he found a
number of books that were in the Latin and
German Old Testaments left over. Jerome
had noticed the same thing long before and
had called these books "Apocrypha"—secret
or hidden books. Luther gave them the same
name and now proceeded to translate them
from the Greek text, except one, Second
Esdras, of which no Greek but only a Latin
version could be found. As we have seen in
an earlier chapter, when he finished his
translation of the Bible in 1534, he put them
in a group by themselves, after the Old Testament. This course was promptly followed by
Coverdale, in the first printed English Bible,
the next year. And thereafter all the great
historic English Bibles followed the same procedure, making these books a separate group,
and putting them after the Old Testament—
the Thomas Matthew Bible of 1537, the
Taverner of 1539, the Great Bible of 1539,
the Geneva of 1560, the Bishops' of 1568, and
the King James of 1611. Only in the Catholic Old Testament of 1610, which was translated from the Latin Vulgate, they remained
scattered through the Old Testament, as they
still are in the Douai Bible of the Catholic
Church.

What were these books, which stood so high
in Christian esteem for so many centuries,

and still form a part of any complete Authorized Bible?

They were partly expansions of Old Testament books, particularly Esther and Daniel, to make them more edifying or interesting. Esther as it appeared in the Hebrew Bible had little or no religion in it. It does not even mention the name of God. But when it was put into Greek, its translators remedied this by introducing a strong religious element into the story. Mordecai and Esther utter long prayers, and the book closes with a religious review of its action.

Daniel too was enriched by three additions —Susanna, Bel and the Dragon and the Song of the Three Children. Susanna, a highly colored tale really meant to effect a reform in Jewish judicial procedure, was sometimes put at the beginning of Daniel, to introduce him to the reader as a young man of extraordinary gifts. Bel and the Dragon are two short stories intended to ridicule idolatry. Both are clearly suggested by narratives in Daniel itself.

Some of the Apocrypha, like Ecclesiasticus, were translations of Hebrew works that have long since disappeared in Hebrew. Ecclesiasticus is the name the Greeks gave to the Wisdom of Jeshua, or Jesus, the son of Sirach, who lived in Jerusalem about B. C. 200. He was a sage, or wise man, and his Wisdom is the longest of all the pieces of such literature that have come down to us. It dealt with a great variety of topics, mostly of a very practical kind, which are handled in a manner far from commonplace. Echoes of this remarkable old book meet us in the Epistle of James, and in the sayings of Jesus, especially those about behavior as a guest, a subject on which Sirach has much to say. He was fully alive to the beauty of nature, and was also a very social being, fond of the company of his fellow men, and very conscious of the duties of friendship, family, and employment. While he glorified Wisdom as among the loftiest of God's attributes and the goal of man's best endeavors, he saw the religious character of man's daily work; he said of the farmer, jeweler, smith, and potter, that "they support the fabric of the world and their prayer is in the practice of their trade" (Ecclesiasticus 38. 30).

Another great piece of Wisdom literature we owe to the Apocrypha is the Wisdom of Solomon, so called because Solomon was the ideal of the sages. It was really written in the reign of Caligula, about A. D. 38-41, when the Jews in Alexandria were undergoing persecution. It had a marked influence upon Paul, particularly when he wrote the Letter to the Romans, and helped to shape his view of Jesus, in whom he saw the embodiment of the divine Wisdom described in Wisdom 7. 26 —compare Colossians 1. 15. The same passage in Wisdom is quoted in Hebrews 1. 3. In

fact, Wisdom seems even to have influenced
the Christology of John (Wisdom 9. 1, 2, compare John 1. 1-3). The influence of Wisdom
upon the Christian doctrine of immortality
is also marked: "God created man for immortality, and made him the image of his own
eternity" (Wisdom 2. 23). While the latter
part of the book is in quite a different key,
the first ten chapters of Wisdom are a gem
of Alexandrian Jewish literature. No wonder
they influenced Romans, Colossians, Ephesians, Hebrews, and John.

Jewish fiction found expression in Egypt
not only in the story of Susanna but in the
books of Tobit and Judith. Tobit was the pattern or model Jew, who resists idolatry,
goes regularly to Jerusalem for the feasts,
not only paying his tithes but spending and
giving liberally, buries the neglected dead,
and scrupulously observes the ceremonial
law. Misfortune overtakes him; he becomes
poor, despised and blind, but at last his con-
stancy is richly rewarded. It all makes a
really famous short story.

Angels and demons play prominent parts
in Tobit, as they do in some of the leading
books of the New Testament. Tobit's concern
to bury Jews killed by the government reminds us of the pious action of Joseph of
Arimathaea, long after, in claiming the body
of Jesus, and giving it Jewish burial, and
helps us to understand it. And Tobit's words

about giving are still heard in some Christian churches unto this day: "If you have little, be not afraid to give according to that little" (Tobit 4. 8). So Tobit held up the old Jewish ideal for the Jews of Egypt. In the earliest *Book of Common Prayer* (1549) Tobias and Sarah, not Abraham and Sarah, were mentioned as the ideal pair. Tobias was Tobit's son.

Judith may be described as a Pharisaic novel. The heroine scrupulously observed the law of foods and washings although shut up in the tents of the enemy's general, whom she was planning to slay, and did slay, thus delivering her people from great danger. The incongruity of her meticulous performance of her religious duties with her ruthless murder of an unconscious man is what gives the story its peculiar quality for the modern reader. Shakespeare named his daughters Judith and Susanna.

First Esdras ("Esdras" is the Greek form of "Ezra") is little more than a combination of parts of Second Chronicles, Ezra and Nehemiah. It is no mere translation, however, but is composed in excellent Greek. The only real addition is the story of the three guardsmen of King Darius, who keep themselves awake debating what is the strongest thing in the world. Their answers are submitted to the king and his courtiers, who agree that while Wine, the King, and Woman are strong, Truth is strongest of all.

The most important historical pieces in the Apocrypha are the two books of Maccabees. They are especially interesting to the New Testament student, as one tells the story of the Maccabean revolt from a Sadducee's point of view, and the other from a Pharisee's.

First Maccabees tells the story of the Syrian king's effort to force Hellenism upon the Jews, and the opposition the Jews offered to it under the leadership of Judas Maccabeus and his brothers. It carries the narrative down to the founding of the Hasmonean house by Simon, the third of these great brothers. It thus forms an invaluable historical link between the Old Testament and the New, and it tells a heroic story. It was written in Hebrew, early in the last century before Christ, and was soon translated into Greek. When the Gospel of John speaks of the feast of Dedication, or Rededication (John 10. 22), it refers to the celebration instituted by Judas Maccabeus when he and his followers had recovered the Temple from the Syrians and resumed the offering of sacrifice in it (1 Maccabees 4. 59).

Second Maccabees, written a few years later, tells the first part of this story, through the recovery of the Temple by Judas, but embellishes it with accounts of dreams, marvels, and angelic appearances. It is plainly Phari-

saic in origin, for its story stops with the
restoration of the Temple worship; that was
all the Pharisees were interested in, and the
further successes of the Maccabean brothers
in making Judea politically independent, the
Pharisee who wrote Second Maccabees left
untold. For him the restoration of the Temple worship was the true climax of the Maccabean revolt.

The terrible story of the Maccabean
martyrs, 2 Maccabees 7, is reflected in Hebrews 11. 35-38.

After the fall of Jerusalem in A.D. 70,
thoughtful Jews came to realize that their
best policy was to acquiesce in the political
rule of the Romans and try to become loyal
and law-abiding subjects of the empire. In
such a spirit of penitence before God and
adjustment to the new conditions, a Jew of
Egypt, about the end of the first century,
wrote the Book of Baruch, under the name
of the friend and secretary of the prophet
Jeremiah (Jeremiah 32. 12, 16, etc.).

The latest book of the Apocrypha is that
extraordinary group of apocalypses of various times known as Second Esdras, because
Ezra plays such a part in it. The six pieces
that make it up date all the way from the
Jewish War, A.D. 66, to the disasters that
overtook the Roman armies in the days of
Decius, Valerian, and Zenobia, A. D. 251 to
270. Resolved into its component parts it

throws light on a number of periods of Christian and Jewish thought and experience, but taken as a unit it perplexes and annoys the reader; Luther himself said of it, in his characteristic bold and vivid fashion, that he "threw it into the Elbe."

Some people who cannot believe that in First Peter or Revelation Babylon means Rome, would find help in apocryphal books like Second Esdras. Baruch, and the Letter of Jeremiah, in all of which Rome is regularly spoken of as Babylon. It was part of the apocalyptic vocabulary.

We are in danger of getting a false view of Jewish and Christian religious history if we try to pass directly from the Old Testament to the New, omitting the Apocrypha. They formed part of the literary background of the Christian movement. They introduce us to the dramatis personae of the New Testament—saints and sinners, Pharisees and Sadducees, angels and demons. Their influence is on every book of the New Testament. Yet perhaps the most instructive thing they have for us is the contrast between Pharisaic and Christian attitudes that they make possible.

For on the last page of the Apocrypha, 2 Maccabees 15. 33, Judas the hero of the Pharisees is hanging up the head of the slain Syrian general before the Temple, and preparing to give his tongue piecemeal to the birds. So wrote the Pharisee. What a contrast to the voice of the gospel: "But I tell you, Love your enemies, and pray for your persecutors, so that you may show yourselves true sons of your Father in heaven."

QUESTIONS

1. Where did the Apocrypha arise?
2. Where did they appear in the Greek, Latin, and earliest German and English Bibles?
3. Where did Luther put them?
4. What influence did this action of his have upon the printed English Bibles?
5. What types of literature are represented in the Apocrypha?
6. What New Testament books show their influence?
7. What great New Testament ideas do they help us to understand?
8. How do they contribute to our knowledge of Biblical history?
9. To what groups familiar in the New Testament do they introduce us?
10. What is your favorite book in the Apocrypha?

CHAPTER VI
THE BEGINNINGS OF THE NEW TESTAMENT

THE first things to be written among the Christians were the letters of Paul. He wrote them to help the people in his new and struggling churches to a sounder view of the new religious experience to which he had introduced them. The problems he dealt with were immediate, local, and sometimes personal, and he handled them directly and vigorously. He had no idea of producing a literature, still less a scripture. His writings were just personal or group letters, designed to produce an immediate practical effect, and then disappear.

And this they did. They were written between A. D. 50 and 62, and then evidently disappeared, for the earliest Gospels, which came out between A. D. 70 and 90, show no acquaintance with them. Paul had a very definite view of Christ; he thought he was the pre-existent Messiah, the embodiment of the divine Wisdom; but neither Mark, Matthew, nor Luke reflects this idea of Jesus. It is evident that Paul's letters were unknown among the churches.

He had, however, told the Colossians to get hold of a letter he was writing to Laodicea (probably meaning Philemon), and to share their own letter with the Laodiceans (Colossians 4. 6). This would naturally have led to the preservation of these two letters in the church chests of both these churches. This step toward the collecting and preserving of his letters Paul himself took, quite unconsciously of course. His purpose in inviting the Colossians to read what he had written to Philemon was to bring to bear the Christian sentiment of the churches of both Colossae and Laodicea to secure the safety of the runaway slave Onesimus, whom he was taking the awful responsibility of sending back to his master Philemon.

Other churches too had letters from Paul, which they were holding, and perhaps occasionally reading aloud in their meetings, but no one seems to have thought of collecting them until about thirty years after his death. His martyrdom would naturally give them a greater appeal, and probably here and there a church would read its letter from Paul on the anniversary of it.

It was not until the appearance of Luke-Acts, with its striking picture of Paul—on his journeys and in his missionary work, before courts and mobs, in the midst of riots and shipwrecks—that anyone seems to have thought of collecting what letters of his could still be found. Indeed, it was probably the account of Paul in the Acts that stirred somebody to hunt up the surviving letters of Paul and publish them.

It is a curious fact that if anyone had Colossians and Philemon to begin with, the Acts would have guided him to all the rest of the letters Paul wrote to churches that have come down to us. So it seems likely that some Asian Christian, perhaps from Laodicea or Colossae, and so possessed of Colossians and Philemon, stirred by reading the story of Paul in the Acts, immediately set about looking for any other letters of Paul that he might have written to the churches mentioned in the Acts.

Certainly someone, soon after the appearance of Luke-Acts, collected and published the letters of Paul to seven churches, probably prefixing to the collection an introductory letter to Christians everywhere (our Ephesians), commending the collection to them as the work of a man who had labored, written and suffered to carry the Christian message among the Greeks (Ephesians 3. 1-11).

This is the explanation of the great rhapsody upon the Christian salvation with which Ephesians begins, chapter 1. You can well imagine a man who had just read the letters of Paul for the first time—the first man who ever read them—breaking out in an ecstatic survey of the blessings of the Christian experience as Paul had described it. No wonder he speaks with such enthusiasm of Paul's religious genius, his great spiritual endowments (3. 3, 4). In Ephesians the Pauline message is presented in general terms, stripped of local contemporary touches. Its aim is to interest Christians generally in the messages of the Pauline letters (3. 3, 4), which had so much to contribute to the greater movement into which Christianity had grown.

That Paul's letters were collected and published after the appearance of Luke-Acts and before the writing of the Revelation is clear from the fact that while Luke, writing in the circle of Ephesus (Acts 20. 17-38) about A. D. 90, did not know them, the writer of the Revelation, writing in the same circle a very few years later (for Domitian, A. D. 81-96, is still emperor), is so impressed with the Pauline letter collection that though he is writing a Revelation he begins it with a group of letters to seven churches prefaced by a general letter to all seven. But all the Christian writing of the following generation shows the influence of Paul's collected letters: the Revelation, Hebrews, 1 Clement, 1 Peter, the Gospel of John, the letters of Ignatius and Polycarp, and a few years later Timothy, Titus, and 2 Peter.

The sudden shower of *letters* of Christian instruction that now descends upon the churches—Revelation, Hebrews, 1 Clement,

1 Peter, Ignatius, Polycarp, John—gives
further evidence of the influence of the Pauline letter collection. It took just this collection of Paul's letters to make the value of the
letter type convincingly clear to Christian
teachers, and led them to adopt it. And not
only is this evident from the widespread re-
sumption of the individual letter as a means
of Christian instruction, but the production
of *collections* of letters shows it even more
clearly—in the Revelation (letters to seven
churches), Ignatius (seven letters), and John
(three letters, one general, one to a church,
and one personal).

From the time Paul's letters were first
collected and published they began to exercise
a powerful influence upon Christian thought
and life, which has never ceased; but it was
to be a long time before they were publicly
read in church as scripture, side by side with
the Old Testament. Yet this collection of
Paul's letters was the first step toward the
New Testament that was to come.

The gospel-writing movement began with
the Gospel of Mark, written in Rome, about
the time of the Fall of Jerusalem in A. D. 70.
The Gospel of Matthew followed, about ten
years later, in Antioch, while Luke's two
volumes, Luke-Acts, probably appeared in
Ephesus, about A. D. 90. But these books,
which we instinctively group together, were
not grouped in that way by the early Church.

Matthew really reproduced Mark, and hence replaced it; fifteen sixteenths of Mark reappear in Matthew, and Luke took over three fifths of Mark. Taking the three Gospels together, between one third and one half of their material is repetition. But they were not intended to go together; each was meant to be used by itself. In fact Luke's Gospel was meant as the first volume of his book on the rise of Christianity.

Early in the second century—about A. D. 110 —a fourth Gospel was written, the Gospel of John. It had become clear that the field of Christianity was the Greek world, and the new Gospel undertook to state Christian truth in a way directly intelligible and attractive to Greeks. It was a bold recasting and restatement of the new religion. A few years after its appearance, it was combined with the other three into a group of four—Matthew, Mark, Luke, and John—and these together presented such a wealth of religious values that no single Gospel could compete with them. Matthew maintained itself for a time as a separate book, but in a few years the fourfold Gospels as a group attained a pre-eminence they have ever since maintained.

This combination of Gospels was not put forth, however, as a scripture; the motive of the collection was at first probably only to further the influence of the new Gospel of

John, by combining it with its older rivals and so winning a hearing for it from those who were attached to this or that one of them. It was for their sheer practical religious usefulness that the four Gospels were prized and circulated in the second quarter of the second century.

A number of books from the second quarter of the second century show acquaintance with the fourfold Gospel—the Preaching of Peter, 2 Peter, the Gospel of Peter, the Interpretations of Papias of Hierapolis, the Epistle of the Apostles, the new British Museum Gospel, and the Apology of Justin. In all these books the Four Gospels are reflected.

On the other hand, Marcion, the shipowner of Pontus, who made such frantic efforts to revive Paul and throw aside the Old Testament about A. D. 140, preferred Luke to the other Gospels. He was the first man to try to formulate a Christian scripture, that is, a body of Christian writings to take the place of the Jewish Bible in Christian worship. Marcion found much in the Old Testament that was repugnant to his Christian moral sense, and so he advocated giving up the Jewish scriptures altogether, and putting in their place in public worship a Christian collection, consisting of the Gospel of Luke and ten letters of Paul. He had a good deal of success in his reorganization of Christian churches on this new basis, but in the end his churches came to be regarded as heretical. The Church was too much attached to the Old Testament to give it up. But his idea of a Christian scripture collection to be read in church survived and helped to shape the movement for a New Testament a few years later. Only when it came, it was to stand side by side with the Old Testament, not in place of it.

Meantime the collection of four Gospels was rising steadily in Christian esteem. When Justin wrote his Apology, about A. D. 150, in Rome, he describes the way in which Christian worship was conducted. He had been converted in Ephesus about A. D. 135, but spent his later years at Rome, where his principal writing was done. The procedure he describes may have been that of both cities, but it was certainly that of Rome in the middle of the second century. Justin says that the brother who presided at the service read "the Memoirs of the Apostles or the Writings of the Prophets" before the congregation, "as long as time permits."

The Memoirs of the Apostles is Justin's name for the Gospels, and it is clear that about A. D. 150, the Church in Rome was reading them side by side with the Prophets (meaning the Old Testament) in Sunday worship. Not, however, the Letters of Paul, which the Roman Christians may have hesitated to use as scripture partly because Marcion had been so strong for them. At any rate, while Marcion and his followers were using Luke and ten letters of Paul in their meetings as scripture, most Christians, certainly those of Rome, were reading the four Gospels side by side with the Greek version of the Old Testament. If these rival groups had been willing and able to combine their Christian scriptures, they would have been well on their way to our New Testament.

QUESTIONS

1. What seems to have led to the collecting of Paul's letters?
2. When and where was it done?
3. What was its purpose?
4. What place did Ephesians have in it?
5. What effect did its publication have upon Christian literature?
6. When were the Gospels first collected?
7. What was the original purpose of their publication as a collection?
8. What innovation in Christian worship did Marcion advocate?
9. What was the scripture in use among the churches as Justin knew them?
10. How would their combined scriptures have compared with ours?

CHAPTER VII
THE FIRST NEW TESTAMENT

THE second century was a time of great
sectarian activity in Christianity. Erratic
types of teaching or practice began to honey-
comb the churches before A. D. 100. After
the mysterious "Nicolaitans" of Revelation
2. 6, 15, came the Docetists, who claimed that
Christ was too divine to suffer, and must
have only seemed to do so; the Gnostics, the
Marcionites, and toward 175 the Montanists.

Some of these sectarian leaders, like Marcion, actually tried to organize and unite
all the scattered churches under their banner,
with their particular doctrines and tenets.
Justin says that when he wrote, A. D. 150-60,
Marcion had great multitudes of followers in
every nation. The danger such movements
constituted to the normal development of
Christianity was even more acutely felt when
schismatic leaders like Montanus made their
appearance in the third quarter of the century. The Montanists professed to be prophets, and to speak under divine inspiration.
Their founder Montanus claimed to be the
Paraclete, the "Comforter," or Helper, of
John, chapter 14. Tertullian became a Mon-
tanist before he died.

In the presence of dangers like these,
Christian leaders, particularly in Rome, un-

dertook to effect a closer organization of the many independent loosely related churches. One plank of the platform on which Roman Christians now sought to unite the churches was a definite Christian scripture, side by side with the Old Testament. Indeed, to oppose Montanism successfully nothing was more necessary than to fix the limits of inspired Scripture, for so many Montanists claimed to be inspired themselves.

This must have taken place toward A. D. 175, for we find this new movement toward organization reflected in three principal sources.

First, in Irenaeus of Lyons, who about A. D. 185 wrote his famous "Refutation of Gnosticism" (literally, "Knowledge falsely so called"), usually called his work "Against Heresies."

Irenaeus came from Ephesus, but he did his work in Lyons, in Gaul. With Tertullian of Carthage and other Christian leaders of his day he felt that the hope of the churches lay in a return from contemporary speculations and isms to the faith of the apostles, and as the only church in the western world that could lay any claim to contact with them was the church at Rome, he pointed to its type of Christianity as the purest and the one to be followed by the churches of the west. It is the fact that men as far apart as Tertullian in North Africa and Irenaeus up in

Gaul both felt in this way about following the lead of the church in Rome, in deciding what was sound Christianity, that makes us think the new movement had its source in that city.

Tertullian wrote his works, mostly in Latin, in the vicinitiy of Carthage, the first center of a Latin Christianity, toward the close of the second and in the early years of the third centuries. A curious fragment of Christian writing called from its discoverer the Muratorian Fragment, is our third witness to the rise of the New Testament, for it actually gives a list of Christian books which may be read publicly in church. This fragment of three pages from some lost early Christian writing, perhaps by Victor of Rome, at the end of the second century, gives the list accepted in Rome itself, about A. D. 200.

All three of these witnesses agree that the four Gospels, Matthew, Mark, Luke and John, may be so read. The four were considered as a unit—the Gospel—one part by Matthew, one by Mark, and so on. The publication of the four together, fifty years before, had so advertised that type of literature that a shower of "apocryphal" Gospels had resulted, but none of these had been able to make much headway against the great quartette, and none ever found a place in the New Testament.

Along with this great collection of early Gospels, went the great collection of ten letters of Paul; these two collections from the beginning of the New Testament formed its main bulk. But the very name of Irenaeus's book shows that there were already added to the Pauline collection what we know as the Pastoral Letters, Timothy and Titus, for it quotes a phrase from 1 Timothy 6. 20, "knowledge [gnosis] falsely so called." Paul's Letters had evidently been enlarged by the addition of First and Second Timothy and Titus, which cleared Paul of any suspicion of favoring Marcionism, by his endorsing the Old Testament (2 Timothy 3. 15-17), and repudiating Marcion's well-known book, the *Antitheses* or *Contradictions* (1 Timothy 6. 20). Irenaeus, Tertullian and the author of the Muratorian fragment agree in enlarging the Pauline letters, from the ten that were in Marcion's list, to thirteen, by this addition of the three Pastorals.

Each of these great collections had long been treated as Scripture in one group or another of Christian churches, but now they are combined, and authorized for use in public worship. At this time too they are united and bound together in a most masterful way by the addition of the second volume of Luke's work, under the name of the Acts of the Apostles. Of course this greatly clarified the historical relation of Paul and his letters to the gospel narrative, but it was added less for its historical interest, which we feel so keenly, than for the service it rendered in filling in the figures of the apostles, which had now assumed a new importance in the controversy with the sects as to what was genuine Christianity and what was not. Everything that could serve to knit up this new scripture collection with the apostles, the personal followers of Jesus, was felt to be important.

A few short letters, bearing the names of Jude, Peter, and John, helped to serve this interest and strengthen the bond between the apostles and the new scripture collection. Irenaeus recognized a letter of Peter, and one or two of John; the Muratorian writer, two of John and one of Jude; and Tertullian, one each, of Peter, John and Jude. On this point the New Testaments of Lyons, Rome and Carthage seem to have varied slightly from one another.

Another point of variation between them was in the matter of Apocalypses, or Revelations. For each of them knew and accepted in his New Testament two revelations: Irenaeus, the Revelation of John, and the Shepherd of Hermas; the Muratorian writer, the Revelation of John and the Revelation of Peter; and Tertullian, the Revelation of John, and for a while the Shepherd of Hermas, though he later repudiated it. The Revelation of Peter was a hideous little work, written A. D. 125-50, describing heaven and hell, and trying to show how the punishment was horribly designed to fit the victim's crime. The Shepherd was a work of Roman Christianity, written about the beginning of the second century, to show the possibility of repentance for sin after baptism, which Hebrews seemed to deny (Hebrews 6. 4-6). The Shepherd taught that one might repent of such sin and be forgiven once, but only once.

Each of these earliest New Testaments adds up to twenty-two books—just the total Josephus says the Jews of his day made of the books of their Hebrew Bible. But this may have been a coincidence. Certainly, the books of the Greek Bible the Christians used in the second century were never counted in that way; they were nearer fifty than twenty-two.

It must also be remembered that the Christians of Egypt included a good deal more in their Christian scriptures at the close of the second century than the Roman Christians did. For instance, Clement of Alexandria counted Hebrews among the letters of Paul, and the Chester Beatty manuscript of Paul's letters (written about A. D. 200) has Hebrews right after Romans, the order being Romans, Hebrews, Corinthians, etc. But it was almost two hundred years before Hebrews was accepted in the west as a letter of Paul's, and so entitled to a place in Scripture.

Egyptian Christianity was inclined to accept as scripture almost anything it found edifyng; it seemed to feel that what inspired was inspired. It was also too easily impressed by claims of apostolic authorship. Clement, who wrote in Alexandria between A. D. 190 and 212, included the Revelation of Peter and the Shepherd of Hermas in his scripture. He also accepted the Letter of Clement of Rome to the Corinthians and the Letter of Barnabas as apostolic. All this seems less strange when it is remembered that our oldest complete Greek New Testaments include most of these curious works, the Alexandrian manuscript (of the fifth century) having the Letter of Clement right after Revelation, and the Sinaitic manuscript (fourth century) having Barnabas and the Shepherd there. So close are these great manuscripts to the usage of Alexandria around the year 200.

While the conflict with the schismatics about A. D. 175 drove western Christianity to formulate its authoritative Christian writings to stand side by side with its Jewish Bible, it is at once evident that most of the books it accepted in the new collection had been in Christian use for a long time, and had been making a place of indispensable usefulness in the life of the churches. What was now done was principally to recognize the place Paul's great letters and the Four Gospels had already made for themselves in

Christian esteem and service. These great bodies of Christian writing are now bound together and supplemented by the Acts of the Apostles, two or three general letters, and one or two apocalypses or revelations.

These are the books that Roman Christianity, along with Gallic and North African, now proposed to accept as authorities on what was Christian and apostolic, and to read in public worship along with the Greek Old Testament. In this period, the last quarter of the second century, the name "the New Testament" (literally, "Covenant or Agreement"), described by Jeremiah and applied in the Epistle to the Hebrews to the Christian religion (8. 8-12), began to be used of this new body of Christian scripture, while the Jewish scriptures were called the Old Testament. Theoretically, they were on an equality as religious authorities, but not practically, for as Harnack once pointed out, the Old Testament is always interpreted to agree with the New, not the New with the Old.

QUESTIONS

1. What sects appeared in the second century?
2. What was the position of the Montanists?
3. What measures did Christian leaders take to protect Christianity?
4. What Christian writers or writings throw light upon this?

5. Why did the western churches follow the Roman church?

6. What did the Roman New Testament contain?

7. How much of this had already been used in public worship?

8. How does it compare with the position of Egyptian Christians at that time?

9. What light do the great manuscript New Testaments throw on the Christian practice in Egypt?

10. How did Christian leaders make a place for their new scripture side by side with their older Greek Bible?

CHAPTER VIII

THE NEW TESTAMENT COMPLETED

THE Roman church and other western churches continued to use this New Testament of twenty-two books for at least a hundred years. Hippolytus of Rome early in the third century accepted it, as did Cyprian of Carthage, in the middle of the century.

But eastern and western Christianity, Alexandria and Rome, were going different ways. Cyprian's contemporary Origen, the great Alexandrian scholar, had a New Testament of a larger pattern. Origen was well aware of the differences among the churches about what should be included in the New Testament, and as he was more a scholar than a churchman, he did not settle the problem, he analyzed it.

Origen divided the books in his own New Testament into two classes—the acknowledged books and the disputed ones. He accepted them all, but he knew that some refused to accept a few of them, and this fact he very fairly admitted.

His "acknowledged" list, containing the books that all Christians accepted as scripture, consisted of the four Gospels, fourteen letters of Paul (including Hebrews), the Acts, two Catholic letters, 1 Peter and 1 John, and the Revelation of John—twenty-two books.

His "disputed" books were: the Letter of James (which no earlier writer had included in the New Testament), 2 and 3 John, 2 Peter, Jude, the Letter of Barnabas, and the Shepherd of Hermas.

The New Testament of Origen, we see, is obtained by combining the accepted with the disputed books, which make twenty-nine books in all, or two more than we have in our New Testament today—Barnabas and the Shepherd. But lest anyone should think this was some slip on Origen's part, this is precisely the contents of the oldest Greek manuscript of the entire New Testament that has come down to us—the Codex Sinaiticus, written about the middle of the fourth century, which ends with Barnabas and the Shepherd.

Seventy-five years after the death of Origen, another eastern Christian, Eusebius of Caesarea, tried to clear up the still vexed question of what should be in the New Testament. Eusebius was the father of church history, and finished his history of the church in A. D. 326. While his discussion of this matter is much less clear than Origen's, it is certain that Eusebius' New Testament was more like ours than Origen's was, for Eusebius omitted the Shepherd and Barnabas. On the other hand, the writings of Dionysius, the bishop of Alexandria, on the Revelation had greatly shaken the faith of the eastern church in that book, and its place was becoming very insecure. What staggered Dionysius was how the same man could have held the views of the Gospel of John and the Revelation of John, or written both books. Modern learning agrees with him entirely in this, and does not attempt to make them the work of the same John. But the eastern church felt that if the Revelation was not by the apostle, it did not belong in the New Testament.

This doubt about the Revelation has always prevailed in the eastern church, and most mediaeval Greek manuscripts of the New Testament omit it; roughly speaking, about twice as many Greek manuscripts omit it as contain it. Other disputed books which Eusebius himself rejected from the New Testament were the Acts of Paul, the Shepherd, the Revelation of Peter, the Epistle of Barnabas, and the Teaching of the Apostles, which some eastern Christians, probably in Egypt, evidently still accepted as Christian scripture.

That these curious works had their advocates about A. D. 300, is shown by the list of books of scripture copied into the Clermont manuscript of Paul's letters now in the National Library in Paris. The manuscript was written in the sixth century, but the list must have been copied from a much older one, for it counts Barnabas among the Catholic let-

ters and includes at the end of the New
Testament, the Shepherd of Hermas, the
Acts of Paul, and the Revelation of Peter.
The same Egyptian breadth as to inspiration
which had so enlarged the Jewish scriptures
in Egypt by the incorporation into them of
the Apocrypha, was at work toward a larger
New Testament than the Roman church
would allow. We have seen how Clement of
Alexandria, about A. D. 200, added Hebrews
to the Letters of Paul, and accepted the Revelation of Peter and the Shepherd of Hermas,
along with the Revelation of John; he also
admitted the Letter of Clement and the
Epistle of Barnabas to his list of Catholic
Epistles; and quoted the Preaching of Peter
and the Teaching of the Apostles as scripture
—making a New Testament of thirty books.
So from the first emergence of a Christian
scripture in Egypt, it was a very inclusive
list.

Another great figure of Egyptian Christianity was Athanasius. He became bishop of
Alexandria immediately after the Council
of Nicaea (A. D. 325) and held that office for
almost fifty years. He was banished to Gaul
for a time, and knew the west as well as the
east. In fact he may be said to have known
the Christian world of his day all the way
from Upper Egypt to Belgium.

It was his custom to issue at Easter a letter
to the churches of his diocese, and in A. D.

367 he took as its subject the books to be read in church. And his New Testament list is exactly like ours today. But he adds the Teaching of the Apostles and the Shepherd of Hermas, as good reading for people receiving Christian instruction in preparation for joining the church. He mentions five books of what we know as the Apocrypha as good for this purpose also—the Wisdom of Solomon, the Wisdom of Sirach, Esther (with the Greek additions), Judith, and Tobit.

It might seem that with Athanasius the contents of the New Testament were at last settled, but diversity of practice continued among the churches of the east and the west. The first Christian teacher of the west to accept Hebrews as Paul's was Hilary of Poitiers, who died in A. D. 367, the very year of Athanasius' Easter letter.

It is interesting to look at other great Christian leaders of the century that followed. The greatest of the interpreters of the New Testament was Chrysostom, the noted preacher and patriarch of Constantinople. His sermons still fill a dozen huge volumes. He came from Antioch, where a shorter New Testament was accepted. His Synopsis of Holy Scripture had fourteen letters of Paul, four Gospels, the Acts, and three Catholic letters. This was exactly the contents of the great standard Syriac version, the Peshitto, which made its appearance in A. D. 411, a few years after Chrysostom's death. Repeated efforts were afterward made to prevail upon the Syrian church to accept a New Testament of twenty-seven books, like that of Athanasius, but without success. Syriac Christianity has always clung to the short Peshitto New Testament.

Chrysostom had an immense influence upon the understanding of the New Testament, and much that is best in many a modern commentary goes straight back to him. But he did not prevail over Athanasius in the conflict over what should stand in the New Testament. Theodoret of Cyrrhus (386-458), who had grown up like him in Antioch, agreed to this shorter New Testament, but another great man of Antioch, Theodore, bishop of Mopsuestia, in Cilicia, had no Catholic letters at all in his New Testament; it consisted of the Gospels, the Acts, and Paul.

Gregory of Nazianzus, in Cappadocia (329-89), one of the four "doctors" of the eastern church (along with Athanasius, Chrysostom, and Basil), accepted four Gospels, the Acts, fourteen letters of Paul and seven Catholic or "general" letters, but no apocalypse. This was and long continued a common form of the New Testament in the east.

Amphilochius of Iconium, who died in 394, accepted four Gospels, the Acts, and fourteen letters of Paul, observing that some omit Hebrews but are wrong about it. "Of Catholic letters," said Amphilochius, "some say seven, others only three—one of James, one of Peter, and one of John." "The Revelation of John some accept, but the majority call it un-canonical." How widely informed Amphilo-chius was!

Meantime the New Testament had been translated into Latin, and in A. D. 382 Jerome, the great scholar of the western church, set about revising it. He visited the east, and spent a long time in Palestine, working upon the Old Testament. He was well aware of the doubts that had prevailed in the west about including Hebrews among the letters of Paul, but he included it in his revised Latin New Testament, although he observed that "the custom of the Latins does not accept it."

Jerome's version, the Latin Vulgate, be-came the standard Bible of Western Europe, and is still that of the Catholic Church. Its New Testament contents were just those Athanasius had listed in his Easter letter of A. D. 367—twenty-seven books, with four Gospels, the Acts, fourteen letters of Paul, seven Catholic Epistles and one revelation, that of John.

The makers of Latin manuscripts were much more successful in putting the whole New Testament into one convenient volume than the makers of Greek ones were. Few Greek Christians in the Middle Ages had or saw the New Testament in one book; usually it made three or four volumes. The more compact and convenient form in which it circulated in the west helped to give definiteness and fixity to its contents, and the immense number of the surviving manuscripts of the Latin Vulgate—something over ten thousand—helps us to understand its victory. There were indeed fluctuations in the contents of the New Testament here and there in the Middle Ages, but in general its contents remained pretty definitely fixed.

This fixity was, of course, made complete by the invention of printing. It was to help in the multiplication of copies of the Latin Bible that printing was invented, and the first books printed with movable types were Psalters or Bibles, of course in Latin. It was probably in 1456 that the great 42-line Latin Bible was printed at Mainz, and from that time the printing of the Latin Bible went on apace. The invention of printing had put the finishing touch to the long process of determining the contents of the New Testament.

QUESTIONS

1. What contribution did Origen make to the development of the New Testament?
2. How many books did his New Testament contain?

3. How did it differ from the New Testament of Rome?

4. How does it compare with the New Testament of the Sinaitic manuscript?

5. How did Eusebius' New Testament compare with Origen's?

6. What led to doubts in the east about the Revelation?

7. What was the New Testament of Origen's predecessor Clement?

8. What had Athanasius to say about the books to be read in church?

9. How did Chrysostom stand on this matter?

10. What position did Jerome take in the Latin Vulgate?

11. What effect did printing have on the whole matter?

CHAPTER IX
THE BIBLE IN GREEK, LATIN, GERMAN AND ENGLISH

WE have seen that the Greek version of the Hebrew scriptures had been the Bible of the early Church. It already contained ten books which were not in the Jewish Bible of Palestine, but which had originated among the Jews of Egypt, who had also produced the Greek version of the Hebrew Bible. These books, which later came to be called Apocrypha, were not separated from the rest of the Greek Bible but were scattered among them.

When Jerome revised the Latin Bible, late in the fourth and early in the fifth century, he noticed their absence from the Hebrew scriptures of Palestine, but did not on that account omit them from his Latin Vulgate version, contenting himself with designating them as "Apocrypha," that is, secret or hidden books. So they continued to stand in the Latin Bible as they had stood in the Greek, scattered among the rest of the books.

The Latin Bible was translated into German in the fourteenth century, and, of course, these Apocrypha were translated as parts of it. So in the numerous printed German Bibles that appeared between 1466 and 1522 and in

the Catholic German Bibles that followed
them, these Apocrypha were included.

They also found places in the first English
Bible of which we know, that produced by
John Wyclif and his helpers, Hereford and
Purvey, in 1382. This Bible was translated
from the Latin Vulgate, and, of course, included the books we call Apocrypha. It assumed two forms, for Purvey carried the
work to a second, revised edition. It circulated in manuscript, of course, and as it was
difficult to own it and not easy to read it, its
success was not very great. The English in
which it was written was also far from that
of the sixteenth century, when the real foun-
dations of the English Bible as we know it
were laid.

A few examples of Wyclif's English will be
interesting.

"Nyl yee deme, that yee be not demede, for
in what dome yee demen, yee schulen be
demede" (Matthew 7. 1, 2). "I am a verrey
vyne, and my fadir is an erthe tilier" (John
15. 1) ; "Sue yee charite" (1 Corinthians 14.
1) ; "Men of Athenes, by alle thingis I se you
as veyne worschipers" (Acts 17. 22) ; "Bilevest thou kyng agrippa to prophetis? I woot
for thou bilevest" (Acts 26. 27) ; "Brethren
nyl yee be made chyldren in wittis, but in
malice be yee litil, forsothe in wittis be yee
parfite" (1 Corinthians 14. 20).

It is often said that there were English

translations of the Bible earlier than Wyclif, but if so they have disappeared without leaving any manuscripts behind. The fact is that, while there are hints here and there of partial translations, covering this or that part of the text, there is no evidence of any complete version having been made before Wyclif, and the evidence for the partial translations is far from sufficient. This silence of the manuscripts is strongly corroborated by the express prohibition by one church authority after another of translations into English. Through the convocation of Oxford in 1408, Archbishop Arundel expressly forbade the translation of the scriptures into English, and the reading of Wyclif's translation, and the preface of the Rheims (Catholic) New Testament version of 1582 frankly admits that such translations have not previously been allowed.

Wyclif was aided in his translation by his pupil, Nicholas Hereford, who did most of the Old Testament. Followers of Wyclif went about the country reading the new Bible to common people who could not read it for themselves; these were the Lollards, whose work, though often cruelly opposed, went on for a century and a half and helped to prepare England for the Reformation.

After Wyclif's death in 1384, his associate John Purvey revised his translation, and it is this revision, completed in 1388, that ap-

pears in most of the extant manuscripts of
the translation, which number one hundred
and eighty. Purvey's version was not *printed*
until 1731, and Wyclif's did not appear in
print until 1848. Of course both forms of the
translation had long before ceased to be of
any practical religious use, for their diction
was out of date and they had been replaced
early in the sixteenth century by the new
translation movement led by William Tyndale.

The defect of all this work of Wyclif and
his men was, of course, that it was based not
on the Hebrew or Greek originals but upon
Jerome's Latin version of these. But in
Wyclif's day it was the best that could be
done, for Greek was a dead language in England at that time, and Wyclif himself, though
he had been Master of Balliol College, Oxford,
could not read it.

It seems to have been Erasmus who called
attention to the need for translations of the
Bible into modern languages, that common
people used and could understand. Church
authorities had long been openly hostile to
translations of the Latin Bible. But when in
1516 Erasmus published the first edition of
the Greek Testament to appear in print, he
wrote in his preface: "I vehemently dissent
from those who would not have private per-
sons read the Holy Scriptures, nor have them
translated into the vulgar tongues. . . . I

would wish all women, girls even, to read the Gospels and the letters of Paul. I wish they were translated into all languages of all peoples."

Certain it is that Luther almost immediately undertook to meet for German Christianity the need Erasmus had pointed out, for in 1522 he produced his translation of Erasmus' Greek Testament into idiomatic German. Luther made great efforts to put the meaning of the Greek New Testament into the current German vocabulary and idiom. His aim was to reach the people with a version that really spoke their language.

Luther esteemed any scripture only in proportion as it "taught Christ." "Was treibt Christus" was his test. So approached, some books even of the New Testament fell far behind others in his esteem. The most backward were Hebrews, James, Jude, and the Revelation. These books Luther could not quite exclude from the New Testament, but he put them together at the end of it, separating them from the rest in numbering the books, so that they appear almost like an appendix. He numbered the others from 1 to 23, but he gave these four no numbers. But all twenty-seven of the books of the New Testament are present, although slightly disarranged.

Luther followed his translation of the New Testament with a translation of the Hebrew

Old Testament, in four parts. These were published at intervals as they were completed. Meantime the German version of the New Testament was circulating by leaps and bounds, going into one printing after another. It is said that eighty-five editions of it appeared between 1522 and 1533, or before the rest of the Bible was finished.

But when Luther had finished translating the Hebrew Old Testament, there still remained a whole series of books that were in the Latin Vulgate Bible, and with one exception in the old Greek Bible, but were not in the Hebrew Bible—the miscellaneous little library Jerome had long before called the Apocrypha. Luther now translated these, and published them in 1534 as the last installment of his complete Bible, which made its appearance that year.

Luther's translation was so well done that it went far to form the basis of German as a literary language; it is generally regarded as the beginning of German literature. It set so high a standard that for centuries no further efforts to translate the Bible into German were made; they seemed superfluous. Even in the past half century, which has witnessed such numerous efforts to translate the Greek Testament into modern English, German efforts at a modern vernacular version have been few and unsuccessful.

Luther's rearrangement of the later books of the New Testament, indeed his depreciation of some of them, influenced Tyndale in his arrangement and treatment of them; in fact, John Rogers, in his Bible of 1537, still follows Luther in putting Hebrews, James, Jude, and the Revelation at the end of the New Testament. Even the Great Bible of 1539 reproduces Luther's order in the table of contents, but interestingly enough abandons it in the table of contents on the New Testament title page and also in the actual arrangement of the books, for Hebrews and James actually follow Philemon, and Jude follows 3 John. That is, Hebrews follows the letter of Paul, James begins the Catholic Epistles and Jude ends them. So the Great Bible arranges the closing books of the New Testament in three different ways, in its table of contents, its New Testament table of contents on the title page of the New Testament, and in the actual printing of the books.

Of far greater importance was the influence of Luther upon the place of the Apocrypha in the English Bible. His procedure in gathering these books together and putting them in a group after the Old Testament was followed by all the early English Bibles, except the Catholic Old Testament of 1610, in which, of course, they were scattered

through the Old Testament, for that version
was made from the Latin Vulgate, and followed it in the placing of these books.

English Bibles continued to print the Apocrypha together, between the Old Testament
and the New, until Puritan repugnance to
many things about them led to their being
quietly dropped from some bindings of the
Geneva Bible. This happened as early as
1599. Even copies of the King James Bible of
1611 began to drop them out occasionally as
early as 1629. But they were still theoretically parts of the complete Bible.

So it was really Luther's influence that led
to the practical dropping of the Apocrypha
from the Bible, for if he had not first
segregated them, the Puritans could not so
easily have eliminated them altogether. Today
there is hardly an English Bible that can be
held in the hand, published on either side of
the sea, that includes the entire Bible, Old
Testament, Apocrypha, and New Testament.
The University Presses of Oxford, Cambridge, and Chicago are the only ones known
to me who have such editions. Yet whether
we like them or not, the Apocrypha form an
integral part of the historic English Bible,
from Coverdale to King James, and for any
thorough literary, esthetic, or religious understanding of the Bible they are indispensable.

QUESTIONS

1. How did the Apocrypha come by that name?
2. Where did they appear in the early Greek and Latin Bibles?
3. Where were they in the first German and English Bibles?
4. Who produced the first English Bible translation?
5. How did the Church regard English translation of the Bible?
6. What use was made of this first English version?
7. From what text was it translated?
8. How did Erasmus feel about modern translations of the Bible?
9. On what did Luther base his translation of the Bible?
10. How did he rearrange the New Testament?
11. How did he rearrange the Old Testament?
12. What led him to do this?
13. What were some of the effects of Luther's translation?
14. What has become of the Apocrypha?

CHAPTER X

THE ENGLISH BIBLE, FROM TYNDALE TO KING JAMES

THE call Erasmus had uttered for translations of the Bible into modern languages was in direct violation of a score of Catholic prohibitions of such efforts, extending over many years. But it found a response in Germany in the heart of Luther, and another in England in the heart of Tyndale.

William Tyndale was a young Englishman of reformation principles, who had studied at Oxford and Cambridge. In his talks with religiously minded people, he had come to the conclusion that it was "impossible to establish the lay people in any truth except the scripture were plainly laid before their eyes in their mother tongue"—"which thing only," he added, "moved me to translate the New Testament."

Failing to find church support for himself while he should make the translation, he went abroad to complete it and began the printing of it at Cologne in 1525. But Catholic agents learned of the enterprise and broke up the work and Tyndale fled to Worms, where the printing was completed before the end of the year.

The translation was made not from the Latin Vulgate but from the original Greek, as published by Erasmus, in his third edition, of 1522. It owed little or nothing to the earlier works of Wyclif and Purvey; "I had no man to counterfeit," says Tyndale, "neither was holpe with englysshe of any that had interpreted the same, or soche lyke thing in the scripture before tyme."

Tyndale's debt to Luther, however, was considerable. Indeed, there is some reason to think he visited the great Reformer, though this is by no means certain.

Copies of Tyndale's translation reached England early in 1526. They were eagerly welcomed by people interested in the Reformation, but rigorously proscribed and sought out for destruction by the church authorities. The result is that only one copy of the Worms octavo is now known to be in existence—that in the Baptist College in Bristol, England.

Tyndale's spelling is very different from ours; in his day there were a dozen ways of spelling "it"; but his language strongly colored all the succeeding revisions of the New Testament, and ninety-two per cent of the King James Version of it is still just as William Tyndale wrote it, more than four hundred years ago. Modern translators find themselves again and again going back to his interpretations, where the standard versions had abandoned them. His work was well done.

He proposed to use the familiar spoken English of his day. He declared that he would make a version a plowboy could read and understand. It was this democratic instinct combined with his scholarly conception of his task and his real literary genius that gave such distinction to the work of Tyndale, and made its influence so enduring.

Tyndale went on to learn Hebrew, and set about translating the Old Testament. His financial backers were a group of English merchants, who held reformed views. He completed the Pentateuch and published it in 1530. But in 1535 his enemies finally overtook him; he was imprisoned near Brussels, and the following year he was executed.

But he had set the English Bible on its way; and it went rapidly forward. In 1535, when Tyndale was in prison, Myles Coverdale put out the first printed English Bible. No one knows its printer's name or even where it was actually published. Somewhere on the Continent; certainly not in England! Coverdale hesitated to tell who had helped his project financially; as he put it, "God moved other men to do the cost hereof." "It grieved me," he wrote, "that other nations should be more plenteously provided for with the scripture in their mother tongue than we."

Coverdale made use of the work Tyndale had done. He used his translations of the Pentateuch and the New Testament. Then as he was unequal to translating the rest of the Old Testament out of Hebrew and the Apocrypha out of Greek, he simply translated the best German and Latin versions that were available, and on his title page frankly described his work as "faithfully and truly translated out of Douche and Latyn in to Englishe."

Coverdale followed Luther, as we have seen, in assembling the Apocrypha and putting them after the Old Testament, a proceeding destined to have great influence upon all subsequent Protestant revisers and translators.

It is surprising how little has been done in Germany in the way of Bible translation or revision since Luther. Luther's Bible was in fact an end. Coverdale's on the other hand was a beginning. Only two years elapsed before another English Bible made its appearance, bearing the name of Thomas Matthew. This is generally believed to have been a pen name for John Rogers, who afterward became the first of the Smithfield martyrs in Queen Mary's persecution in 1555.

John Rogers had been Tyndale's last friend, and possesed his translation of the first half of the Hebrew Old Testament, from Genesis to Second Chronicles. He also had Tyndale's last revision of the New Testament. His Bible was therefore half the work of Tyndale. For the rest of the Old Testa-

ment, and for the Apocrypha, Rogers simply
revised Coverdale's translation, which as we
have seen was made from German and Latin
versions. But the fact that one half of the
new Bible was actually translated directly
from the original Hebrew and Greek made
it a great improvement upon Coverdale's,
especially from Joshua to Second Chronicles.

The feeling of English churchmen about
the Bible in English had by this time so far
altered that Archbishop Cranmer now wrote
to Cromwell, King Henry's prime minister,
asking him to secure a license from the king
for Rogers's Bible, and so it became the first
licensed English Bible, and could be bought
and sold, owned and read, without danger of
molestation by the authorities. The English
Bible had won its victory over the State.

But the victory over the Church remained
to be won, and two years later the English
Bible won that victory too. For the John
Rogers Bible in the short space of two years
became the basis of two other English Bibles;
one, a revision made by one Richard Taverner, and published in 1539, and the other,
the famous Great Bible, which appeared
in the same year.

The Great Bible was called Great because
it was a huge book, intended to lie on a
church lectern or pulpit; it was what we
call a "pulpit Bible." And this was the most
notable thing about it, for now for the first

time Englishmen began to hear the Bible read in church not in Latin but in English, the language they could all understand. In the Great Bible the English Bible won its second great victory, the victory over the Church.

For it was a church Bible. Cranmer and the bishops had at last agreed that there must be an English Bible for use in public worship, and they invited Coverdale to revise the John Rogers Bible for such use. And so arose the first Authorized English Bible. For that is what "authorized" means, as applied to the Bible—authorized by the church authorities for use in public worship.

The Great Bible was such a big book that no London Printer could produce it, and so the job was sent to the Royal Printer in Paris. But there the Inquisition stepped in and broke up the work. Whereupon Coverdale, who was supervising it, quietly reassembled printers, presses, type and printed sheets in London, and after that books of such size could be printed there.

The Great Bible was warmly welcomed by the English religious public. In every parish church a copy of it was set out, to be read by anyone who wished to do so. It was secured by a chain so that it could not be stolen, and so the Great Bible became the famous Chained Bible of English church history. But it was chained not to prevent its being read but to facilitate it. Many grown people learned to read, it is said, in order to read the English Bible, which now for the first time was made really accessible to them.

About the middle of the sixteenth century two things happened of great importance for the English Bible. One was the making of the *Book of Common Prayer*, which appeared in 1549. It contained the Psalms in English, for reading and chanting in church, and of course this Psalter was taken from the Authorized Bible, the Great Bible of 1539. And so it comes about that to this day the Psalter in the Prayer Book is the Psalter of the Great Bible, as first translated and then revised by Myles Coverdale.

The other event of those years was the invention of the verses. These four early Bibles had no verse numbers or divisions. They had the old Vulgate chapters divisions that went back to the twelfth century. But it remained for Robert Etienne, the French printer, to devise the verse numbering of the New Testament, which he introduced into his 1551 edition of the Greek Testament. He was making a concordance of the Greek Testament and needed a more convenient unit of reference than the old chapters, clumsily marked off with A, B, C, and so on, in the margin every ten or twenty lines. Unfortunately, Etienne made every verse a paragraph, and this led people to think each verse had the completeness of a proverb, which was very far from true.

His ingenious system was speedily adopted by the Puritan refugees in Geneva, who were busying themselves with the revision first of the New Testament (1557) and then of the Bible (1560).

The Geneva Bible was a book of moderate size, about ten inches in height—obviously not a pulpit but a fireside Bible. It was printed not in the old black-letter, but in the elegant new Roman type, which was just coming into fashion—the type that is in universal use today. It was broken into the convenient verses so recently introduced by Etienne, which so regrettably interrupted the sense; and it was enriched with marginal notes of which its makers said that they did not believe there was left one passage in the whole of scripture the meaning of which was not made plain!

The Geneva Bible, generally known as the Breeches Bible, because it reads in Genesis 3. 7, "and they sewed figtre leaves together, and made themselves breeches," had a great history. It passed through more than a hundred editions; it was the Bible of Shakespeare, of Cromwell and his Ironsides, of the Pilgrim Fathers and the Mayflower Compact. It was the basis of Cromwell's Soldier's Bible. It was also an important contribution to a better English Bible, for its makers knew

Hebrew and Greek, and were able to make much needed improvement in the translation of the second half of the Old Testament and of the Apocrypha.

It was soon followed by a revision of the Great Bible. Englishmen heard that Bible read in church, but at home they read the smaller Geneva Bible, with its convenient little verses. So Archbishop Parker organized a revision of the then Authorized Bible (the Great Bible), and in 1568 appeared the second Authorized English Bible, called the Bishops', because so many bishops worked on the revision. It was rather hurriedly done, for a group of books would be assigned to one man, and he revised those books as he saw fit. The new Bible took over the verse division of the Geneva Bible. It was, of course, a pulpit Bible, a tall stately massive volume, though smaller copies of it was soon issued, for private use.

English Catholics had no English Bible as yet, but in their English College then at Rheims, in France, one Gregory Martin in 1578 set about the translation of the Latin Bible into English. He proceeded, it is said, at the rate of two chapters a day, and completed the whole Bible within four years. Only his New Testament was immediately published, however. It came out in 1582, the Old Testament (including the Apocrypha) waiting until 1610 for its publication. By that time the College had removed to Douai, so that the whole translation came to be called the Douai Bible. It was often revised, the last time by Doctor Challoner, in 1749, but a new revision is said to be now under way.

The climax of all this great period of Bible translation and revision was reached when in 1604 King James summoned a conference of high and low churchmen to consider "things pretended to be amiss in the church." In the course of the discussion, John Reynolds, president of Corpus Christi College, Oxford, the leader of the Puritans, moved that they retranslate the Bible. King James took up the suggestion and named the committees or companies to which the work was referred. And so arose in 1611 the King James Version, a very cautious revision of the Bishops' Bible of 1568. It was the third authorized English Bible.

English had made great advances as a literary language since Tyndale published his New Testament in 1525; Shakespeare and the Elizabethans had done their work; and this progress is to some extent reflected in the King James Version. It is certainly a standard piece of English literature and a treasure of Christian liturgy and it brought the heroic period in the history of the English Bible to a noble conclusion.

QUESTIONS

1. Who responded to Erasmus' call for modern language translations?
2. When did the English New Testament first appear in print?
3. How was it received?
4. What further work did its translator do?
5. What became of him?
6. Who produced the first English Bible to appear in print?
7. Who was John Rogers, and what service did he render to the English Bible?
8. To what further Bibles did his work lead?
9. What is meant by the "Authorized Bible"?
10. How many can you name?
11. What part of the Great Bible is still preserved in the Prayer Book?
12. Describe the Geneva Bible.
13. Who produced the Catholic English Bible?
14. What led to the King James Version?
15. What is its chief value?

CHAPTER XI

MANUSCRIPT DISCOVERIES AND PRIVATE TRANSLATIONS

ONLY a few years after the appearance of the King James Version (1611), there was brought to London (in 1628) a Greek manuscript of the Bible which made a deep impression upon English scholars. It was sent to the king, Charles I, by the Patriarch of Constantinople, Cyril Lucar, and contained the Old Testament in the Septuagint Greek version together with the Greek New Testament. It was called the Codex Alexandrinus, the Alexandrian manuscript. It was written in the fifth century, and its great antiquity claimed attention for the text it contained. It is now one of the chief treasures of the British Museum.

Other manuscripts of almost equal age had been brought to France or England, and English scholars came to feel that in them a more ancient and original text of the New Testament was to be found. This conviction resulted in a series of efforts on the part of individual scholars to translate this more ancient text into English, and it introduced a new and usually forgotten chapter in the story of the English Bible.

One of the first of these private translations was that of W. Mace, published in

London in 1729, along with a Greek text of
the New Testament, described as "the original text corrected from the authority of the
most authentic manuscripts." A few years
later, in 1745, William Whiston, the translator of Josephus, published his Primitive
New Testament, translated directly from the
three leading Greek manuscripts then known,
at Cambridge, London, and Paris. William
Whiston was professor of mathematics at
Cambridge, having succeeded Sir Isaac New-
ton in that position.

In 1775 John Wesley published his translation of the New Testament. It was entitled
"The New Testament with Notes, for Plain,
Unlettered Men who know only their Mother
Tongue." It has had an extended influence,
especially among English Wesleyans. In
1789-91 Gilbert Wakefield, a Cambridge
scholar, published a vigorous translation.
Archbishop Newcome published a new version in 1796, in Dublin.

In America, Charles Thomson, who as secretary of the Continental Congress had written its records in his own hand, translated
the whole Greek Bible, and the Old Testament from the Septuagint version, and the
New from the original Greek, in 1808. This
was the first English translation of the Septuagint, which was afterward independently
translated in England by Sir Lancelot Brenton, in 1844. It is curious that both Thomson

and Brenton omitted the Apocrypha from their translations. Thomson was influenced to make his translation by a letter from his friend, Thomas Jefferson.

In 1826 Alexander Campbell revised and published at Buffalo, Virginia, the New Testament translations of George Campbell, James MacKnight, and Philip Doddridge, and this version, "The Sacred Writings," was widely used by Campbell in his religious and educational work. In 1833 Noah Webster, whose speller and dictionary were so influential, produced a revision of the Bible, designed to correct and modernize its diction.

Meantime the New Testament manuscripts that were coming to light were necessitating thorough revision of the Greek text of the New Testament, and a series of revised editions of the Greek New Testament brought their testimony home to New Testament students everywhere. The famous Vatican manuscript of the Greek Bible, written in the fourth century, was coming to be recognized as the soundest of our sources for the New Testament text. Between 1850 and 1870 this progress in manuscript study was particularly marked. And the new knowledge of the original ancient text was steadily reflected in new English translations.

While manuscript discoveries were numerous, they were particularly dramatized by Tischendorf's discovery in 1859, in a convent

on Mount Sinai, of the Sinaitic manuscript.
It contained the whole New Testament, including Barnabas and part of Hermas, and
about a third of the Old, and like the Vatican
manuscript, was written in the fourth century. This magnificent discovery made it
impossible to disregard the bearing of Greek
textual progress upon the English Bible, and
led in 1870 to the action of the Convocation
of Canterbury, the southern half of the
Church of England, in undertaking to revise
the Bible.

Meantime English textual scholars like
Alford and Tregelles were hard at work,
and Westcott and Hort had begun their
revision of the Greek New Testament. In
America, Catholic and Protestant scholars
had published revised translations of the
New Testament, the Catholic, of course,
based upon the Latin Vulgate text, not on
the Greek. It was Archbishop Kenrick who
produced this Catholic revision, in 1846-51.
Between 1842 and 1869 very competent work
was done in America in revising or retrans-
lating the Greek New Testament by Ken-
drick, Norton, Conant, Anderson and Noyes.

The English Revisers accepted American
cooperation, and under the leadership of Dr.
Philip Schaff an American Committee of Revisers was organized, which exchanged readings with the English Company through a
series of years, and had a limited influence

upon its deliberations. One of the leading rules of the English Revision was in any changes they might feel compelled to make, to use diction as old as that of King James or older. Their language was consequently no more modern than that of the text they were revising; it was if anything even more antique. But they did make some progress in reflecting the new knowledge of the more ancient and original text which for the New Testament at least the manuscript discoveries had brought to light.

The *Encyclopedia Britannica* states that the work of the revisers was received without enthusiasm; but this is certainly an understatement. It is said that three million copies of the Revised New Testament were sold within a year of its appearance. Two days after the book arrived in New York on May 20, 1881, it was printed in full in both the Chicago morning papers of the time in their daily issues. "No such reception," says Dr. P. Marion Simms, in *The Bible in America*, "was ever accorded any other book in the history of the world." The Old Testament was published with the New in 1885, and the Apocrypha appeared in 1894.

But while the revisers were at work and even after they had finished their revision, private translations continued to appear. In 1876 Julia Smith published at Hartford, Connecticut, and the Old and New Testaments, translated from the Hebrew and Greek but unfortunately marred by her grave misunderstanding of Hebrew syntax. Ferrar Fenton published a translation of Paul's Epistles in Modern English, in London, in 1883, evidently feeling that the antique diction of the standard versions obscured the meaning. His complete New Testament appeared in 1895, and in 1900 he published the Old and New Testaments together. His New Testament was based upon the Greek text of Westcott and Hort, and his forceful modern English gave back much of its original vigor to the New Testament. His work has gone through many editions.

The propriety of basing translations upon the Hebrew and Greek originals has come to be felt by Catholic scholars, and London Jesuits have recently completed the New Testament part of what they call the Westminster Version of the Sacred Scriptures, made not from the Latin Vulgate but from the Greek text, and are proceeding to translate the Old Testament from the Hebrew.

While Greek manuscripts of the New Testament as old as the fourth, fifth, and sixth centuries were available for the textual study underlying the revised New Testament, and scholars like Tischendorf, Tregelles, and Hort gave many years of patient investigation to their study, no such wealth of Hebrew manuscripts has come to light for the Old

of the University of Michigan. The manuscript of the Gospels and Acts comes from the first half of the third century; it is, unfortunately, much damaged. That of the Revelation covers almost one third of its text; it comes from the third century.

Seven Old Testament books are represented in the collection, some of them by extended bodies of text, notably Genesis. These Greek Old Testament manuscripts date from the middle of the second century after Christ to the fourth.

Before biblical learning had been able to absorb these new materials, another startling find of great antiquity was disclosed when, in 1935, Mr. C. H. Roberts reported the discovery in the Rylands Library of a little fragment of the Gospel of John in a hand earlier than A. D. 150. This piece, torn from a leaf book possibly as old as the time of Hadrian, is the oldest evidence we have of the existence of the Gospel of John—older than any mention of it in Christian literature.

So thick and fast are the discoveries coming of more and more ancient manuscripts for the recovery of the original text of the Old and New Testaments. When peace returns to the world and travel and excavation are again possible, we may expect still greater results for the textual study of the Bible.

But already manuscripts discoveries in

very different fields have had such a profound effect upon New Testament translation that they require a special chapter for their study.

QUESTIONS

1. What important manuscript was brought to England soon after 1611?
2. Why did such discoveries stimulate new translations?
3. Name some leading examples of such efforts in England.
4. What was done in this direction in America?
5. What great manuscript discovery attracted most attention?
6. To what important action did it lead?
7. How was this work received?
8. Did interest in biblical translation subside with its appearance?
9. How does our present stock of New Testament manuscripts compare with that used by Erasmus?
10. What recent discoveries have added to our manuscript resources?

CHAPTER XII

THE GREEK PAPYRI AND THE MODERN SPEECH TRANSLATIONS

WHEN Bishop Lightfoot was a young professor at Cambridge in 1863, he once said to his students, as one of them recorded in his notes, "If we could only recover letters that ordinary people wrote to each other without any thought of being literary, we should have the greatest possible help for the understanding of the language of the New Testament generally."

There seemed very little likelihood of such a wish being gratified, but as a matter of fact Greek papyri were already beginning to come to light in the sands of Egypt, and these discoveries, which have since swelled to a veritable flood, have shown that the young scholar of thirty-four was abundantly right. He would, in fact, have been amazed at the depth of the truth of his remark.

For the Greek papyri are more than ninety-five per cent nonliterary; they are documents of common life: deeds, leases, contracts, complaints, notices, letters, invitations, accounts, lists—every kind of business and private paper you can think of and hundreds you would never think of, all written in familiar, everyday Greek, the vernacular Greek of New Testament times.

It was a young German pastor, Adolf Deissmann, who while looking over some recently published Greek papyrus documents one day in the Heidelberg library, in the early nineties, was struck with the likeness of the Greek in them to that of the New Testament. He saw as fact what Lightfoot thirty years before had forecast. The New Testament is written in colloquial Greek, the plain speech of common life, the language the papyri are written in.

It was this discovery that precipitated the wave of modern speech translations of the New Testament that has marked the past forty years. Of course we should have been prepared for it, for every great translation has had the ordinary reader in view, and has tried to use the language of common life. Tyndale declared his purpose of making a version the plowboy could understand, and the King James revisers said in their Preface that the Bible ought to be understood "even of the very vulgar." It is said that Luther visited the meat-markets to learn from the butchers the exact German words in common use in his day for the various parts of the slaughtered animals, so that his translation of the sacrificial ritual of the Mosaic Law would be perfectly intelligible to every German reader.

But long before Luther and Tyndale, Paul himself had in First Corinthians expressly disclaimed a literary style. The Corinthians had complained that he was inelegant in his use of Greek ("rude in speech," 2 Corinthians 11. 6; see also 1 Corinthians 2. 1, 4), and he readily admitted it, declaring that he had no use for the graces of rhetoric, and would not resort to them. Paul has been telling us all along that he wrote plain, vernacular Greek, and the papyri have shown that he meant what he said.

The Gospels, it has long been recognized, were written not in literary Greek but in the ordinary spoken Greek of their day. They were, in fact, the first books to be published in that style.

The papyri have solved a long-standing problem of New Testament study—the strange quality of the Greek employed in it. For it is not classical Greek, nor translation Greek (like the Septuagint), nor even the literary Greek of the first century; it stands apart from all these, and the older German learning went so far as to say that it was "a miracle language, devised by Divine Providence for the purposes of revelation." The papyri have put the clue to the mystery into our hands. The distinctive quality about New Testament Greek is its colloquial character: this discovery, anticipated by Lightfoot and made by Deissmann, has been steadily confirmed and buttressed by the papyrus dis-

coveries of the past half century. And upon
it all New Testament grammarians agree.

This discovery of the vernacular character
of New Testament Greek may be compared
with another discovery equally important in
the Old Testament field. For while professor
of poetry at Oxford, 1741-44, Robert Lowth
detected and pointed out the principle of
parallelism that underlies Hebrew poetry, a
matter obviously of great importance for the
understanding of the Old Testament, especially the prophets, almost all of whom were
poets. We cannot blame the makers of the
sixteenth- and seventeenth-century English
Bibles for printing prose and poetry alike,
for they knew no better. But it is strange
that the Revised Versions, English and
American, still treat the great poet prophets,
Isaiah, Micah, Amos, Nahum, and the rest,
as prose! It is as though we were to print
Shakespeare in solid columns of prose. Nothing could more completely disguise their literary character and obscure their meaning.

Another discovery of the greatest importance for the study of the Bible was made
in the nineteenth century, when the new
science of comparative philology completely
transformed the study of language, Greek
and Hebrew included. The decipherment of
hieroglyphic and cuneiform in the same century made it possible to read the ancient
records of Egypt, Babylon, Assyria, and

Persia, and rolled up the curtain on ancient history, so that the historical, literary, and religious background of the Old Testament came clearly into view.

This wealth of new knowledge about the languages and the records of the Bible gradually found its way, of course, into introductions, commentaries, and dictionaries, but at length it overflowed these channels and found expression in new translations. Lowth's discoveries about Hebrew poetry had been partially taken advantage of in the Revised Old Testament of 1885, but the New Testament revisers of 1870-81 were still under the impression that the New Testament, like so much of the Old, was written in the "high" or literary style.

But within twenty years the papyri had shown that this view was altogether mistaken; indeed, they had convinced many scholars that revision was not enough; the New Testament at least must be entirely re-translated, if justice was to be done to its real vernacular character. For if the New Testament was written in a familiar informal style, it could obviously be best translated in that style. Indeed, any other style of translation would disguise it, for it would seek to improve on the style of the apostles and evangelists.

It is from this conviction that the flood of modern speech translations has come. A

Catholic scholar, Father Spencer, translated the Gospels from Greek into familiar modern English in 1898, Cardinal Gibbons saying in the preface, "He has endeavored to represent our Lord and the Apostles as speaking, not in an antique style, but in the language they would speak if they lived among us now." Father Spencer went on to translate the rest of the New Testament, and completed it before his death in 1913, but it was not published until 1937, twenty-four years later, and almost forty years after the appearance of his Four Gospels.

The Twentieth Century New Testament of 1899-1900 resulted from the difficulty ordinary British readers, young and old, found in breaking through the stiffness of standard "Bible language" to the meaning. It was the work of a group of earnest religious people who had seen the necessity of an intelligible English New Testament, and though not trained New Testament scholars they produced an excellent translation.

The same need had impressed Chaplain F. S. Ballentine in this country and he had begun what he called "A Modern American Bible." Two small volumes of his New Testament appeared in 1899, and the complete New Testament in 1902.

Doctor Weymouth's New Testament in Modern Speech was published in 1903, after his death, with funds provided by men who had been educated at his Mill Hill School, in England. It was described as an idiomatic translation into everyday English. Fresh translations continued to appear from year to year, mostly in the United States. But another notable British version was that of Dr. James Moffatt, "The New Testament, A New Translation," which came out in 1913.

Yet Dr. Ernest A. Bell, of the Night Church, in Chicago, so keenly felt the need of a form at least of John that his public could understand that he made and published a translation of it himself in 1922. The feeling was growing among religious workers that the standard forms of the English Bible were not in plain enough English to serve their needs. This was reflected in C. F. Kent's "Shorter New Testament," of 1918, a selection of the more important parts of the text, clothed in a new and vigorous translation.

Renewed activity on the part of American workers found expression in 1923 in Professor W. G. Ballantine's Riverside New Testament, "a translation from the original Greek into the English of today." In the same year Mrs. Montgomery published the first volume—the Gospels—of her Centenary New Testament, and I produced "The New Testament, and American Translation." I felt as Chaplain Ballentine had felt long before that if we are to be in earnest about the colloquial character of the Greek New

Testament, a really colloquial version will be one thing in the British Isles and another in the United States, for vernacular English differs so much in the two countries. There are more readers of the English Bible in this country than in any other, and the time seemed to me to have come for a frank and direct translation of the Greek New Testament into our modern spoken American English. We take great pains to provide Asiatics and Africans with special versions so that they may read the Bible each in his own tongue wherein he was born; and why not do as much for our own young people, and our fellow citizens generally?

In the years that followed, new translations especially of the Gospels have been numerous. Ray Allen published his "Mark" in 1927, and James A. Kleist, a Catholic scholar, his "Memoirs of St. Peter, or the Gospel according to St. Mark translated into English Sense-lines," in 1932. Father Spencer's New Testament, completed before his death in 1913, was published in 1937.

These are only a few of the retranslations of the New Testament since 1900, all of them in the direction of more idiomatic modern English which it is hoped may make on the modern reader some such impression of simplicity, directness, and vigor as the Greek New Testament made on its ancient readers. With their aid it is now possible to read the books of the New Testament, in particular, as coherent units, as they were written to be read.

The new light on Hebrew, ancient history and the Old Testament generally had also led to new translations, though these were naturally not so numerous. In 1917 the Jewish rabbis of this country published a translation of the Holy Scriptures, or, as we call it, the Old Testament. Doctor Kent's "Shorter New Testament" of 1918 was followed a few years later by his "Shorter Old Testament," with new translations of the Old Testament selections, completing his Shorter Bible. Books of selections from the Bible have been numerous ever since Edmund Calamy prepared "The Souldier's Pocket Bible," for the use of Cromwell's army, in 1643. One of the more recent was produced by an English Catholic, Ronald Knox, "The Holy Bible, Abridged and Rearranged" (London, 1936).

Professor Moffatt published a new translation of the Old Testament from the Hebrew in 1924 and 1925, later united with his New Testament to form a Bible. My colleague, Dr. J. M. P. Smith, led a group of thoroughly trained Semitic scholars in translating the Old Testament (1927), and their Old Testament version combined with my New Testament appeared in 1931, as "The Bible—an American Translation." In 1938 I published a new translation of the Apocrypha, the first,

I was surprised to find, that had been made throughout directly from the Greek text (except for 2 Esdras, not extant in Greek), though some individual books had here and there been translated from the Greek by modern scholars. This enabled us to publish in 1939 a really complete modern translation of the whole Bible, Old Testament, Apocrypha, and New Testament—the full contents of the King James and all six of the great English Bibles of the sixteenth century.

So the past quarter century has witnessed fresh translations into modern English not only of the New Testament, but of the Old Testament and even the Apocrypha, all aimed at providing the modern American reader with more accurate, forceful, and intelligible versions. This movement is not at an end, but should and will continue, seeking steadily to keep the Bible reader abreast of advancing knowledge of it. Whatever their literary levels, they have distinguished poetry from prose and once more made possible the coherent and understanding reading of the Bible, not as detached verses but as continuous books.

QUESTIONS

1. What light have the Greek papyri thrown upon the language of the New Testament?

2. What effect has this discovery had upon New Testament translation?

3. What discoveries of the eighteenth and nineteenth centuries have thrown new light on the Old Testament?

4. Name some leading New Testament translations made in Britain in the past forty years.

5. Name some made in America in this period.

6. What new versions of the Old Testament have appeared in the past twenty-five years?

7. What progress has been made with the Apocrypha?

8. What particular values have these modern versions that do not also belong to the standard ones?

9. What do they suggest as to the general attitude toward the Bible today?

10. How wide has the interest in translation been, in terms of creed, communion, and denomination?

CHAPTER XIII
REVIEW AND SUMMARY

RELIGION has been described as the life of God in the soul of man. Long before the Old Testament was written, or even begun, men had felt its power. But it remained for the Hebrew prophets of the eighth century before Christ to make their spiritual discoveries of the justice, the love, and the holiness of God and to set them forth in unforgettable terms. Further advances in religious experience and intelligence found expression in the work of prophets, psalmists, and sages, culminating in the life and teaching of Jesus. It is this literature of religious discovery that we cherish in the Bible.

We have seen how the Jewish scriptures gradually gathered about the first sacred book of the Hebrews, known to us by its Greek name of Deuteronomy; how Deuteronomy first grew into the Law, and then there were added to it the Former and Latter Prophets, including such historical books as Samuel and Kings. Later still, a whole literature of piety and devotion—hymns, prayers, proverbs, and reflections—came to be thought of as sacred too, and to this fact we owe the preservation to our times of these masterpieces of religious thought. For all the rest of Hebrew literature has perished.

The Jewish religious genius found further expression, principally in Egypt, in a series of religious writings, history, wisdom, and fiction, never accepted as scripture by the Jews of Palestine but dear to the early Church, and known to us as the Apocrypha. These Greek books, along with the books of the Hebrew Bible, which had been translated into Greek, formed the Bible of early Christianity, and as it spread into Coptic and Syriac circles in the east and Latin circles in the west, it passed into those languages.

Meantime Christianity had created a special literature of its own, not deliberately, but incidentally in the course of the work of the Greek Mission—the spread of the new faith through the Greek-speaking world. That world was not a distinct geographical area, but interpenetrated Antioch, Egypt, Asia Minor, even Rome itself. In carrying the gospel to that Greek public Christians wrote letters, then Gospels were written, historical books, revelations in the old apocalyptic style, sermons, open letters to Christians everywhere. Christians read the Jewish scriptures in their public worship and soon began to read the Gospels along with these; then the letters of Paul, and then as the rise of the sects forced the Christian churches to define what they stood for, a New Testament. Not at first as long a New Testament as we know, but one of the twenty-two books; but in the centuries that followed, the example of the eastern churches which acknowledged eight or nine other books as scripture led the west as well to the fuller New Testament we know.

The great Greek Bibles of the fouth century, when at last Christianity was free and could build churches and be openely practiced, have the Apocrypha scattered through the Old Testament, and even add some books —Barnabas, Hermas, First and Second Clement—to the New. These last soon fell away, but the fuller form of the Old Testament, amounting to forty-nine books, passed on from the Greek Bible into the Latin and other ancient versions, and finally into the first German and English versions of it. It was Luther who first separated the Apocrypha out from the Old Testament books that stood in the Hebrew Bible, and put them in a group after the Old Testament in his great German version of 1534, and the makers of the first printed English Bibles followed his example. But before 1600 the Puritans began quietly to drop them from their Bibles, and by 1629 copies of the King James Bible of 1611 began to omit them. Now they are seldom found in English Bibles of any kind, though their importance for understanding the New Testament is very great.

In order to serve the cause of practical religion among the common people of England, Wyclif made a translation of the Latin Vulgate in 1382, and John Purvey revised and improved it soon after. This was before the days of printing, of course, and naturally these versions existed in comparatively few copies, and it was difficult to get permission to own one. They had little influence on the printed English Bibles which appeared in such profusion when the Reformation movement reached England, early in the sixteenth century. Luther had published his German New Testament in 1522, and William Tyndale began the new English Bible with his admirable translation of the New Testament in 1525. Zwingli's German Bible came out in 1530, and Luther completed his Bible in six parts, in 1534. The following year Coverdale brought out the first printed English Bible, building as far as he could upon what Tyndale had already accomplished, and supplementing it with the study of Latin and German translations.

The zeal of the Reformers for an English Bible and for an ever better one produced four such Bibles within four years. Coverdale was followed in 1537 by Rogers, and he two years later by the Great Bible and by Taverner (1539). Rogers' Bible was the first licensed English Bible, but the Great Bible was the first Authorized. Now at last Englishmen heard the Bible read in church in a language they could all understand.

The Geneva Bible of 1560 was the first to

break the Bible into verses, and to print it in attractive modern type. It made many valuable and admirable improvements in translation, especially in the parts which had before been translated only from the Latin and German—the Apocrypha and the second half of the Old Testament. As that half included Job, the Psalms and the prophets, this improvement was of great importance. Its Lord's Prayer reappeared fifty years later almost word for word in King James; the latter simply omitted "even" and "also," and accepted Geneva's correction of Tyndale's "trespasses" to "debts."

The Bishops' Bible of 1568 was undertaken as a revision of the Great Bible, and clearly preferred its readings to those of the Geneva Puritans. But the King James revisers—for the King James Version is only a revision—gave much more weight to the Geneva Bible than the Bishops had done, although the king himself had said that he considered it the worst of all the English versions that he knew of. If we compare the Bishops' with its immediate predecessors, the Great Bible and the Geneva, its leaning toward the Great Bible is manifest; which is perfectly natural, for it was undertaken as a conservative revision of the Great Bible. But if we compare the King James of 1611 with its immediate predecessors, the Geneva (1560) and the Bishops' (1658), it shows a marked prefer-

ence of the Geneva readings. And yet it was
designed to be a very conservative revision
of the then Authorized Bible, which was the
Bishops'.

Nowhere perhaps is the influence of Geneva upon King James more marked than in
the names of the prophets, Esai, Jeremie,
Osee, Abdias, Micheas, Sophonia, and Ag-
geus (of the Bishops') becoming Isaiah, Jeremiah, Hosea, Obadiah, Micah, Zephaniah,
and Haggai, under the influence of the Gen-
neva. This was, of course, simply a part of
the better Hebrew learning the Puritan
revisers had brought to bear upon the Old
Testament, of which Bishop Horne and Bishop Grindaɪ, who edited those parts of the
Old Testament for Archbishop Parker in
1568, had not been ready to take advantage.

A close comparison of King James with the
Geneva and the Bishops' shows also how little
that was new in translation it contains. Its
makers were almost invariably satisfied to
choose between the renderings they found already printed in one or the other of those versions. They were in fact revisers, and only in
the most attenuated sense can they be called
translators at all. The generally very slight
touches which they contributed to the text,
however, were often very effective; as when
the Bishops' reading "Greater love hath no
man than this: that a man bestow his life
for his friends," became in King James,

"Greater love hath no man than this, that a man lay down his life for his friends." On the other hand, John 3. 16 stands in King James exactly as it stood in the Bishops' and the Great Bible.

In the King James Bible the first great period of English translation reached its climax. That period had coincided with a great outburst of English literary expression to which the English Bible contributed and by which it also greatly profited.

The King James revision, the third Authorized English Bible, was several times revised in minor ways in the years that followed—1615, 1629, 1638, 1762, 1769—and multitudes of slight improvements in the way of correcting the numerous misprints and improving the spelling were tacitly made. A few obsolete words, like sith and fet, were weeded out. Meantime the discoveries of more and more ancient manuscripts of the New Testament and advances in the study of language and history stimulated new translations especially of the New Testament on the part of individual scholars. Tischendorf's discovery of the Sinaitic manuscript focussed attention upon these, and led to the English Revision begun in 1870, which resulted in the Revised New Testament in 1881, the Old Testament in 1885, and the Apocrypha in 1894. The American Committee which cooperated in the work left behind a selection of readings which were embodied in the American Standard Version of 1901. The publisher, Thomas Nelson and Sons, undertook to turn over the copyright, after two copyright periods of fourteen years should elapse, to some undenominational religious body, and in accordance with this agreement the copyright was turned over in 1930 to the International Council of Religious Education. The Council turned to the theological seminaries for advice and on the strength of it organized a group of fifteen revisers, the American Standard Bible Committee, which has been at work with some interruption since that time. It is hoped that their work of revision will be completed in two or three years more.

Fresh manuscript discoveries continued to be made, the most recent a group of papyrus leafbooks from the third and fourth centuries—the Chester Beatty papyri. And private translations have come out in increasing numbers, especially since the study of the innumerable papyrus documents found in the past fifty years has revealed the colloquial character of New Testament Greek, and called forth the numerous modern speech translations. These translations go so far toward clarifying the meaning of the New Testament that they have largely taken the place of the one-volume commentaries.

The Apocrypha too have shared in this

modern intensification of interest in the
Bible, so that now the entire Bible in its
widest scope is available to the American
reader in translations that take the fullest
advantage of the advances of modern learning. This concern to keep the great messages
of the Bible unescapably before the modern
reader in translations that need not be read
as verses but in which the individual books
can be read as coherent wholes, shows no
sign of abating, but promises to continue and
to develop a much fuller understanding of
the messages the Bible was written to convey
than the standard versions with their mis-
leading verse divisions, their tendency to
word-for-word translation, and their antique
phraseology can now afford.

QUESTIONS

1. What has the Bible to do with religion?
2. What stages can be traced in the growth of
   the Jewish scriptures?
3. How did the Apocrypha arise?
4. What use did the early Church make of
   these collections?
5. What Christian writings were first associated with them in Church?
6. What religious movements further influenced early Christianity to define the
   precise limits of its scriptures?
7. What did Luther do with the Apocrypha?

8. Who made the first English translation of the Bible?

9. When was the English Bible first printed?

10. Name the six English Bibles that followed.

11. What precipitated the Revision of 1881-1894?

12. Tell the story of the American Standard Version.

BIBLIOGRAPHY

Bewer, Julius A., *The Literature of the Old Testament in Its Historical Development*. New York, Columbia University Press, 1922.

Oesterley, W. O. E., *An Introduction to the Books of the Apocrypha*. New York, Macmillan, 1935.

Westcott, Brooke Foss, *History of the Canon of the New Testament*. New York, Macmillan, Seventh Edition, 1896.

Price, Ira M., *The Ancestry of Our English Bible*. New York, Harpers, Ninth Edition, 1934.

Wild, Laura H., *The Romance of the English Bible*. New York, Doran, 1929.

Sypherd, W. O., *The Literature of the English Bible*. New York, Oxford University Press, 1938.

Milligan, George, *Here and There Among the Papyri*. London, Hodder and Stoughton, 1922.

——, *The New Testament and Its Transmission*. London, Hodder and Stoughton, 1932.

Simms, P. Marion, *The Bible in America*. New York, Wilson-Erickson, 1936.

Goodspeed, Edgar J., *The Story of the Bible*. Chicago, University of Chicago Press, 1936.

——, *The Story of the Apocrypha*. Chicago, University of Chicago Press, 1939.

——, *An Introduction to the New Testament*. Chicago, University of Chicago Press, 1937.

——, *The Making of the English New Testament*. Chicago, University of Chicago Press, 1925.

——, *The Formation of the New Testament*. Chicago, University of Chicago Press, 1926.

——, *Christianity Goes to Press*. New York, Macmillan, 1940.

TRANSLATIONS

The Holy Scriptures according to the Masoretic Text; A New Translation. By Max L. Margolis and others. Philadelphia, Jewish Publication Society of America, 1917.

The New Testament in Modern Speech. By Richard Francis Weymouth. Boston, Pilgrim Press, 1903; Revised Edition, 1924.

The Holy Bible: A New Translation. By James Moffatt. New York, Doran, 1926.

The Bible, An American Translation. By J. M. Powis Smith and Edgar J. Goodspeed. Chicago, University of Chicago Press, 1931.

The Apocrypha—An American Translation. By Edgar J. Goodspeed. Chicago, University of Chicago Press, 1938.

The Complete Bible, An American Translation. (The Old and New Testaments and the Apocrypha.) By J. M. Powis Smith and Edgar J. Goodspeed. Chicago, 1939.

INDEX

139

Study the Bible with the help of these
well-known scholars . . .

What The Bible Says

A Systematic Guide to Biblical Doctrine
Edited by Lewis Drummond

Foreword by Billy Graham
In a day when Bible study is so vital to so many,
this concise study makes an excellent companion
for those who seriously consult scripture for
answers to life situations. Scripture topics are
grouped under three sections: The Trinity; Man,
Sin, and His Salvation; and The Church and
Its Service. Contributors are well-known
evangelical English scholars. *Index.* $5.95

*"Without hesitation, I commend this volume
highly to everyone serious about personal faith"*
                                   —Billy Graham

Introducing the Bible

William Barclay

One of the most beloved and best-known expositors
of the Bible in Great Britain helps make Bible
study easier for all who wish to understand the
Word. His writing is nontechnical, and his
thorough coverage makes the world of history,
literature, and wisdom in the Bible one of the
most exciting challenges life can offer. The book
covers the Old and New Testaments and the
Apocrypha. Paper, $1.75